To Omma and Appa

Acknowledgements

ALL THE WORLD'S A STAGE. THIS BOOK would not have been possible without the cast of quirky, delightful and inspiring actors who have shared the stage with me over the years. They are, after all, the stuff of which this memoir is made.

Behind the scenes, however, a number of individuals, in their own way, helped shape the script and its aesthetics. Thank you to my mom and dad for (especially my mom) enduring my endless list of questions about the past – the questions sometimes coming fast and furious in the middle of the night – and for rekindling memories that had slipped into the nether regions of my brain. I am indebted to my editor and childhood friend, Barth Beresford, whose incisive eye and subtle stylistic touch was a game changer. I thank Chongdong Sunim and Robin Armstrong for reading early versions of the manuscript and offering their invaluable feedback and words of encouragement. A 45-degree bow of the head to Nanda Lwin, Steven Tomlins, Albert Lim, Bomook Kim, Heejeh Choi, Dr. Suwanda Sugunasiri, Don Burrell, Kyuhoon Cho, Peter Beyer, Dr. Daniella Shmuel and Heesun Choi for their helpful comments and suggestions on various sections of the book. I thank my former co-worker and "younger brother" Jong Woo Nam for his fact-checking help in South Korea. Thank you to Jamie JungYoon Choi for her eye-catching cover design and for making me look so distinguished in the illustrations, and thank you to Mehdi Sadeghi for taking the back cover photo of me. I am grateful to the late Todd Huddleston, who always "had my back" during the writing process, which encouraged me more than he will ever know. Finally, I thank my publisher, Karma Yönten Gyatso, for agreeing to take on my book, for the elegant artistic touch he lent to the book's overall design and for his patience, which I am sure I tested in the proof review process.

Disclaimer

THE FOLLOWING STORIES ARE BASED ON my memories. I have reconstructed the dialogue and settings that constitute these memories as faithfully as possible. Some events, however, have been compressed for dramatic purposes. Also, some names have been changed to protect the privacy of the individual or because I do not, unfortunately, remember them, as important as the people behind the names are.

Beginning, Middle & Zen

Tales from Canada to Korea and Back Again

Glen Shakwon Choi

BEGINNING, MIDDLE & ZEN
Tales from Canada to Korea and Back Again
Glen Shakwon Choi

Book design by Karma Yönten Gyatso
Cover design and illustrations by Jamie JungYoon Choi
Edited by Barth Beresford

Published by
The Sumeru Press Inc.
301 Bayrose Drive, Suite 402
Nepean, ON
Canada K2J 5W3

Library and Archives Canada Cataloguing in Publication

Choi, Glen Shakwon, 1972-, author
    Beginning, middle & Zen : tales from Canada to Korea
and back again / Glen Shakwon Choi.

Includes bibliographical references.
ISBN 978-1-896559-37-7 (softcover)

    1. Choi, Glen Shakwon, 1972-. 2. Zen Buddhists--Canada--
Biography. 3. Zen Buddhism--Korea (South). I. Title. II. Title: Beginning,
middle and Zen.

BQ946.H65A3 2018   294.3'927092   C2018-902104-7

For more information about The Sumeru Press
visit us at *sumeru-books.com*

Contents

Part I
Old World, New World

1
Layers

T̲h̲e̲y̲ ̲s̲a̲y̲ ̲t̲h̲e̲ ̲J̲a̲p̲a̲n̲e̲s̲e̲ ̲a̲r̲e̲ ̲b̲o̲r̲n̲ ̲S̲h̲i̲n̲t̲o̲ but die Buddhist. In my case, I was born Canadian, but I was about to die Korean.

That's what I was reading in the typed Korean letter clutched in my right hand. I re-read it to be sure. Yes, the South Korean Military Manpower Association (MMA) got the first part of my situation right: I was currently a resident of Seoul. But, no, not as a Korean citizen. I was a foreign student here, a Canadian citizen, born and raised in Toronto. The proof was in my passport.

Yet the notice implied otherwise: since I was a male of a certain age, I was required by Korean law to complete the compulsory military service of 26 months and sign up within about 30 days. And if I didn't have a valid reason for not reporting, I could be facing up to three years' imprisonment.

When I put the folded piece of paper down, the specter of death loomed in my mind like a greying sky. I imagined the country just up the road, North Korea, attacking the South during my service, improbable as it was. But I lost my eldest uncle, my father's oldest brother whom I never met, to the North during the Korean War (1950-53). And I remembered a 38-year-old John F. Kennedy Jr. passed away earlier this year in a plane crash. Was our family afflicted with the Korean strain of the Kennedy curse? my mind veered. I could be thrust onto the front lines and – bam – I'd be yesterday's obituary in the Korean papers: "A Canadian who came to South Korea with pen and notepad at the ready, eager to study Buddhism in graduate school. Died shortly thereafter, with rifle and grenade in hand and bullet wounds to his chest, fighting for the motherland. R.I.P. Postscript: his service to the South was accidental."

I had heard horror stories from my native Korean friends who had done their time. It was a veritable hell on earth, most confided to me while rolling their eyes. Especially if you had a superior who didn't like you. Lots of beatings and bullying.

There were suicides, too. There was the odd person, however, who said you come out of the experience a real man.

I called my mom in the evening, which was morning time in Toronto. I didn't want to alarm her, especially in the middle of her breakfast, so I tried to tiptoe my way into the news.

"Omma, I might have to join the Korean army!" I said, in Korean, after all.

"What!?" she said, almost choking on her food. "What are you talking about?"

"Did you know I'm also a Korean citizen?" I said.

"But how?"

"I don't know. I received a notice from the Military Manpower Association in the mail today. I must be a Korean citizen."

I heard her talking with my father in the background, in hushed and muffled tones.

"It must be because your name is on the family register," she finally said.

"You mean the Choi clan family register?" This was one of the documents I was required to submit whenever I extended my visa. I never questioned why. To me, it was just a quaint memento of my paternal family's lineage.

"It was your grandfather," my mom said, "who reported your birth to the Korean authorities. He was still living in Korea at the time, you see, before he later joined us in Canada."

"So the family register is basically a citizenship document?" I said.

"It must be," she said.

I had lived on this planet for 29 years but never realized I was a dual citizen the entire time.

Before hanging up, I reassured my mom I would call the MMA and get this resolved as soon as possible. I said this in a confident voice, even though I was nervous. I was intimidated by the thought of confronting what I imagined would be an Old School military type, someone who walked around the office in his fatigues and barked in monotones. They also spoke in Korean, which was my second language, which proved too cumbersome whenever I had to speak to matters foreign to me. Unlike my talks with Buddhist friends, I didn't have the specific vocabulary in my back pocket to quickly draw on.

Ding-dong-deng. The subway doors opened, and I stepped inside. The velvet red bench seats were lined with commuters drifting in and out of sleep. Others slumped their shoulders as they leaned on the hanging straps. Another Monday, another long corporate workweek, their body language said. It was 9:15 a.m., and the worst of rush hour was over. I was relieved I didn't have to push other commuters' backs to sardine myself in, before the doors closed. Everyone here did it without a second thought, but I never got used to it. Maybe that was the polite Canadian in me protesting.

I walked over to the doors on the other side and leaned against the metal railing. I looked up at the map of the Seoul subway system on the board above the doors. The eight color-coded and crisscrossing subway lines and their multiple extensions could get confusing. From a certain distance, the map looked like someone had grabbed a handful of entangled colored strings and pasted them against the board. I suppose that's what happens when you have over 10 million people living in one city, I thought.

I took out the wallet-sized subway map from my pocket and compared. Yep, get off at Daebang station, line 1, walk from there to the MMA building.

My body swayed side to side as the subway rumbled along. For a few minutes, I thought about the Buddhist text I still had to translate into Korean for this week's graduate seminar. The dam in my head then broke. A wave of reality swept in. The possibility that I was riding the train to compulsory military service – and thus hell – was real, and my fate would be decided within the next hour.

I thought about my clothes. I made sure to wear the appropriate dress today. A pair of navy blue cotton khakis, albeit a well-wrinkled pair – I had forgotten to iron them – replaced my usual faded jeans, and I tucked my clean white polo shirt into my pants. I also had to start thinking more seriously about what I was going to say to the MMA official I was scheduled to meet.

Once I arrived at the building, I was met by the officer in charge of my file (and life). We both bowed, shook hands and walked to his office. He was a taller middle-aged man with a conservative haircut and a pen clipped to the chest pocket of his white Oxford short-sleeve shirt.

We walked into an open-concept space where several people sat typing away at their desks. The officer sat down at his desk and grabbed a yellow file folder at the top of a pile of papers.

"So," he said, leaning back in his chair, "you said on the phone that you should be exempt from military service?"

"Yes, that is correct," I said. "I'm a Canadian citizen, here on a student visa."

He leaned forward and flipped open the file folder. "That doesn't matter. It shows here that your name is on a family register. You are also a Korean citizen."

That was such a narrow and technical way of looking at things.

"Well, I didn't know that. I was born in Canada, and my grandfather was the one who reported my birth."

The officer continued staring at my file. "I see you're currently a graduate student."

"Yes."

"If you refuse to report, you'll be deported from the country immediately, and you will not be allowed to complete your studies."

I was actually relieved to hear this; I thought he might say they could confiscate my Canadian passport and deny my right to leave the country.

"But why won't you serve in the military?" the officer continued. "You're of Korean blood, aren't you?"

I knew where he was going with this. I had heard this before. Korean blood is thicker than the Canadian water I drank growing up, was what he was saying. In that moment, I regretted being able to speak Korean. The combination of that and my Korean face made me look like your average Cho. If I had an English-y,

Korean-as-a-second-language accent, as I did upon arrival in the country nine years earlier, he probably wouldn't have brought up the blood issue. It was obviously too late to try that tactic now.

I had to think of another approach. And fast.

"Yes, but what has Korea done for me?" I said. "I grew up entirely in Canada. If anything, I should be risking my life to go fight for the Canadian military. I owe Canada everything. I received all of my education there, until now. I'm who I am because of Canada. My parents are there, and they pay taxes there … That's my true homeland." I surprised myself. I didn't know I had that kind of spiel in me, one that spilled forth from the heart.

The officer paused.

"You make a good point," he said. His face broke into a smile, revealing he was somewhat impressed by my heartfelt speech.

He told me to step outside for a moment while he discussed the matter with his colleagues in the department. I waited for several minutes, pacing back and forth in the hallway.

The office door opened. "Okay, please come back in."

"Here's what we'll do," the officer said, sitting back down at his desk. "You don't have to leave the country. But you will have to immediately delete your name from the family register. Go to the Ministry of Justice to do this."

There was a spring in my step as I walked out of the building. I stopped for a moment at the top of the concrete steps at the entrance, looked out into the wide streets of Seoul and exhaled. I got my life back, and I could now re-focus on my studies. Life was so much simpler when I was a kid.

2
Stardust

Once upon a time, there lived a young village girl in Korea named Shim-Chung. She grew up without a mother because the latter died soon after Shim-Chung was born ...

My mom put down the book she was reading to give my older sister and me a gentle pat on the chest. It was around 8 p.m., and she was catching her breath. She had just come up from watching the cash downstairs at Crosstown Discount Variety, the corner store my parents ran, while the helper received a delivery. She then came back up with Heejeh, my 1-year-old baby sister – who was strapped to my mom's back with a blanket – and tucked her in bed, before coming to our room for our almost nightly bedtime story.

I sank a little deeper under the covers, feeling sad for Shim-Chung. I stole a glance at the bed to my left. My older sister, Nuna, didn't flinch. I'd be as strong as her in two years, I told myself, when I turn seven.

My mom sat up straight on my bedside, looking at the both of us with her soft almond-shaped eyes. She was telling the story in Korean, a language we could understand but not speak.

What's more, she continued, Shim-Chung's father was blind, and every day he would make his rounds through the village, begging for food. When Shim-Chung became older, she tended to her father's every need.

One evening, the father went out for a stroll when, suddenly, he slipped and fell into a stream. A Buddhist monk who was passing by in that moment jumped into the water to save him.

"Thank you, sir," the father said.

The monk could tell the man was blind.

"Elderly man," the monk said, squeezing water from the sleeves of his robe. "If you are able, donate 300 sacks of rice to the Buddha. You will then be able to see again."

"Thank you," the father said, bowing his head. He promised the monk he would do his best, although in his heart he knew this would be impossible.

Nuna interrupted. "Omma, why will rice help the father see again?"

"Ah, *geuh guh nun*," my mom said, turning serious for a moment and switching to English, "rice not important, how honest his heart to make donation, can make eyes better."

Shim-Chung heard about her father's conversation with the monk. She became very excited. "I am going to find a way to raise the money to buy the rice," she vowed.

One day a group of men was walking through the village market. "We are looking to buy an unwed woman to sacrifice to the Sea King!" one of them announced.

When Shim-Chung heard this, she knew it was a sign. She rushed over to the entourage and offered herself in exchange for 300 sacks of rice. The men agreed and promised to deliver the sacks to the village temple.

The father tried to stop his daughter, but it was too late. The boat had already set sail with Shim-Chung in it. In the middle of the sea, the crewmen shouted, "Let this girl be our sacrifice to please the Sea King!"

Shim-Chung then plunged into the turbulent waters, where she sank and sank until she reached her new home, the sparkling palace of the Sea King.

Years passed. The Sea King became very impressed with Shim-Chung during this time. "You have a very pure heart," he told her.

So he decided one day to set her free and return her to the earth. He wrapped her in a brilliant life-sized lotus flower and floated it up to the surface of the sea, where the same boat crew who sacrificed Shim-Chung discovered it. They managed to haul in the floating lotus, the likes of which they had never seen before. The crew decided this would make a perfect gift for their young emperor, who was adored across the land.

Upon peeling away the long slender petals of the lotus, the emperor discovered Shim-Chung tucked away inside. He was astonished to see such a beautiful woman. He wanted to make her his wife.

The married couple lived their days in endless luxury and comfort, although the emperor sensed that something was bothering Empress Shim-Chung.

"I once had a blind father. In order to return his eyesight, I volunteered to be sacrificed to the Sea King, who then sent me back here."

The emperor was touched and vowed to find the father for his wife. He ordered his governors to invite each and every blind person across the kingdom for a grand feast in the capital city of Seoul.

Shim-Chung went every day to the banquet hall, but her father wasn't there. She was fast losing hope. On the final day of the feast, she went to the hall to look one last time. She saw an old man across the room that looked like her father, but he appeared much more haggard and older than she remembered him. She approached the man and asked him a couple of questions. When he said his name and told her his background story, she knew it was him.

"O Father, it is I, Shim-Chung!"

"Is it really you, Shim-Chung? My daughter? You were alive this whole time?"

The father burst out crying. And the moment he did was the moment he could see again.

"And that is the end," my mom said, her voice trailing off. Her almond-shaped eyes now drooped to the sides.

"Okay, *ijae ja-ra*. Go sleep."

My mom turned off the lights. I turned my head to the side, away from Nuna, and closed my eyes, wearing a dreamy smile. Shim-Chung's story was so cool, I thought. I hope I can be a part of a miracle like that for somebody important in my life one day. And the Buddhist monk, so wise and mysterious. My thoughts then grew blue and cloudy and my smile wider. I couldn't wait for my sweet dream to start.

3
Go East, Young Man

Overtime. Five minutes left on the clock. Entangled hockey sticks hacked away at the stained tennis ball bobbing up and down on the pebbly road. The clickety-clack of clashing sticks echoed into the ether and ricocheted around the neighborhood homes.

I envisioned Wayne Gretzky in that moment. He was a hockey player, visionary and figure skater rolled into one: Wayne could predict where the puck would go before it actually arrived and then spin and pirouette on a dime with it when it did. *Be Gretzky*, I told myself.

I returned my focus to the road hockey game. I stood off to the side of the crowd of players, my mouth open, tongue dry, eyes on the ball. Suddenly the ball squirted free and right onto my stick. My legs immediately changed course. Two steps and I was in full flight. The stitching lining the ends of my white T-shirt flapped in the wind. One defenseman stood in my way. I dropped my left shoulder but skedaddled to my right the very next instant. I flew around the defenseman with the ball on my backhand.

From the corner of my eye, I saw the goalie loosen the grip on his stick. My instincts took over, and I knew my next move before I made it. The goalie lunged forward with a poke check, but I tapped the ball to my forehand the second he did. Between the goalie's right leg and the left post now lay a foot of gaping space with only white meshing visible in the backdrop. I tapped the ball one last time, after which it rolled into the meshing and nested there, like a billiards ball into a corner pocket.

I stopped and raised my stick high in the air with my right hand. I looked back at my teammates and flashed a wide grin. I was the happiest 10-year-old in the world because we just won pro hockey's most coveted prize – the Stanley Cup – thanks to my overtime goal.

I high-fived Andrew and Ari, who were on my team.

"It's gettin' late," Andrew said, sweat streaming down his temple. He hauled the two hockey nets onto his beefy shoulders. "My mum wants me home for supper now."

"Okay, see ya at school tomorrow," I said.

"Later," I said as I blanket-waved to Chris, Chris' younger brother and Sean, who were on the opposing team.

"Later," they said in unison.

We went our separate ways, Andrew right next door to the two-story red brick house on the corner and Chris and his brother to the grey mansion with the two garage doors diagonally across from Andrew's. Ari had to walk halfway up the hilly road on the other side to get to his place. I had to walk down Heddington to the end of the block, toward the main busy street of Eglinton Avenue, where I lived on top of Crosstown Discount Variety.

As I walked home, the cool spring breeze caressed my shirt. The back of my neck felt sticky from the dried sweat. It was close to 6 p.m., but the sun was still out. The Toronto skies were normally darker by this time in the winter. I glanced over with pride at my Wayne Gretzky-replica Titan hockey stick in my right hand, which swung up and down by my side. It had a left-handed curved blade even though I was a natural righty. For the past year, for hours on end, I had practiced shooting tennis balls against the red brick wall of Crosstown Discount with a left-handed hockey stick, so I could eventually shoot the same way Wayne did.

I opened the door to my house, took off my shoes and ran up the carpeted stairs, sometimes jumping two steps at a time. I saw my mom cooking dinner through the kitchen hatchway to my far right. She saw me come in.

"Deenuh ready, *sone ddak arah*," she hollered over the sound of running sink water.

"Okay," I hollered back. I stuck my neck out past the grandfather clock to my immediate right. Nuna and Heejeh were sitting on the sofa watching their favorite after-school TV shows. I headed back to my room to take my socks off, then to the bathroom to wash my hands and face. I couldn't get the rhythm of the road hockey game out of my head, even after splashing water on my face. The flow of turns, stops and dekes was hypnotic and addictive.

I came out of the bathroom and began to slide my feet along the oat-beige carpet as if it was ice. Our house might have been one floor, but it stretched two homes length-wise, which was perfect for pretend-playing hockey. I visualized myself as the second coming of Wayne Gretzky. I was a professional hockey player in the National Hockey League (NHL), a slight-bodied David up against a team of Goliaths. I kish-kished through the carpet with my back hunched over, slithered snake-like through the imagined maze of opposing players, wiggled past imminent body checks untouched and lit the lamp easily and often. Size may help, but Wayne taught me a great mind and slippery body were invincible.

Yeah, but his *face*, I reminded myself as I stood up straight. Bummer. Big bummer. In the back of my mind, I knew that was the one hurdle I could never overcome. Wayne had sky-blue eyes, a sharp and prominent nose, and long flowing blonde hair. My eyes were black, my nose flat and round, and my hair a spiky straight and black. He had All-Canadian good looks, while there was no category for me. *Damn.* I wanted to look like him, too.

I thought about it for a second. I'm going to be a Glayne Choisky …

"Glen! Moooove!!" a voice suddenly said. I looked over to my right to see Nuna bopping her head. Half of my body was standing in front of the TV.

I had one particularly bad game when I was 12 years old. I was playing for the Warren Park Eagles, a single-A minor ice hockey team in the Metro Toronto Hockey League. On the drive home, my father was silent, his jaw clenched and eyes squinting in discomfort. I sat in the back seat and stared out the window. I could hear the humming noise of the car engine, which was punctuated intermittently by my father's heavy sighs. The silent treatment was deafening.

"*Nah-cham,*" my father finally said. "Why do you put jersey in pants like that!? You not Geuretzky. It looks terrible. *Geuman hae.* No more." One of Wayne's fashion trademarks was to tuck the right side of his jersey into his hockey pants.

"Okay …" I said, barely managing to aspirate the "k."

"And why you so scared of ko-nuhs? You have two eggs in pocket, both is okay!"

My father was paraphrasing a criticism that Harold Ballard, owner of the Toronto Maple Leafs, once leveled at Toronto's Swedish import forward Inge Hammarstrom. Ballard chided Hammarstrom for shying away from the hitting and rough stuff in the corners so much that he could carry eggs in his pocket and never crack any of them the whole game.

Yes, I didn't like getting hit in the corners. It hurt my chest, shoulders and head, even with the shoulder pads and helmet on. My head would jerk back, my veins bulge and my neck muscles strain to hold my head in place when I got hit. And that jolted the fun right out of hockey.

Two years later, when I was 14 and playing for the Goulding Park Rangers single-A team, my father had seen enough. He sent me to Mr. Lee, his old military buddy from Korea who was a judo instructor, to straighten me out. Mr. Lee taught judo classes twice a week at the local Korean Protestant Church.

My younger cousins John Hwang and Peter Choi joined me. They, too, played hockey, and their dads apparently thought their older brother/brother-in-law had the right idea about building mental toughness. Mr. Lee often picked on my cousins and me. When we practiced judo flips with a partner, he would motion me, Peter or John to be his partner, after which he proceeded to flip us as though an Olympic gold medal hung in the balance. When it was time to spar, he would pair me with Peter, who was already my height despite our 4-year age gap. He did it to test our levels of cold-bloodedness and ruthlessness. He wanted to see us throw aside any warm and fuzzy feelings we had for each other as family, by flipping, strangling and slew-footing each other in the name of competition.

"*Geuman!*" Mr. Lee said to Peter and me in the middle of one particular sparring session. "Come heyuh."

"Yes, sir," we both replied. We walked over to him panting and with sweat streaming down our cheeks.

"If you don't try, this is what you get," Mr. Lee admonished the rest of the class as he squeezed together either side of the collar of my white judo uniform with his swollen battle-hardened hands. He then lifted me off the ground. My eyeballs bulged out of their sockets. I stopped thinking in that moment. I couldn't think. Because I couldn't breathe.

After a few seconds, he let go, and I fell to the mat. It was then Peter's turn. When Mr. Lee let us loose on the sparring mat again, Peter and I lunged and grabbed at each other's uniforms like bloodthirsty animals. Lesson learned.

"No. *An dwe.* You have to go judo class," my father said one Wednesday evening as his tall and gangly frame stood over me in the living room. He looked almost offended by the idea.

I hadn't missed a single class for two months, so I thought I had earned the right to skip judo just this once.

"But *Wayne Gretzky's* ... playing tonight," I said in an almost whisper.

"How did you get ticket?"

"I bought it ... at Maple Leaf Gardens ..."

"No. You have to go judo. The hockey game is just exhibition, *ah nee ya?*"

I was lost for words. I had risked life and limb to go downtown yesterday after school to buy a ticket from a seedy scalper standing in front of the Gardens, where the Edmonton Oilers were coming to town for an exhibition game against the Toronto Maple Leafs. "Tickets here! Get your Leafs-Oilers tickets!" I had given the man my allowance money to buy it. This was going to be my first time seeing Wayne play live.

"*Mah-nee muh-guh-ra,*" my mom said, urging me to eat up as she served my father and me an early dinner of steaming white rice, hot bean sprout soup, and an assortment of vegetable side dishes that were sprawled out over the center of the table.

"You hab to eat a lot por judo tonight," she said.

I put a spoonful of the soup into my mouth. It tasted like mud. I was seething inside. I was going to miss the most important event in my life because I had to do something I hated doing? I stayed silent in front of my father, however, because I was scared of him.

After dinner, I went to my room to pack my uniform. I took the thin rectangular Leafs ticket out of my pants pocket one last time and ran my thumb over its grey and white cardboard surface. The surface was as smooth as the ice that Wayne would be skating on tonight, and I wouldn't be there to witness it. My fingernails then grinded against the coarse white fabric of my judo uniform as I stuffed it into my gym bag. I strapped the bag over my shoulder and lugged it downstairs and out the door, where my father was warming up his dark-blue wagon, the Pontiac Parisienne. I opened the rear door and sat in the back seat, directly behind him.

"Are you mad that you can't watch Wayne?" my father said in Korean as he pulled out of the driveway.

His voice had softened. I was taken aback. He must have felt a little guilty.

"Yes …"

That "yes" triggered the tears. I couldn't stop them. They kept flowing and flowing as I hunched over and silently buried my face in my hands. I didn't want my father to see me crying.

"It's okay, only one game. You hab many chance to see Geuretzky …" he said, peering at the rear view mirror. He must have heard me whimpering.

That wasn't the point. I wanted to see him *today*.

We arrived at the church 15 minutes later.

"Okay, hab a good lesson, my son! I pick you up when you finish." I could tell he was trying to cheer me up.

"Okay," I said, my voice cracking.

I stepped outside and closed the car door behind me. With swollen eyes and a sniffling nose, I made my way to the church basement and into an area enclosed by partitions. I saw Peter and John and a few of the other Korean students changing into their uniforms. Seeing my cousins cheered me up. The three of us were close, and they always reminded me of the good old days, when we would fake WWF-wrestle on our couches as kids.

"*Hana … dool … saet*," Mr. Lee roared.

We started to warm up on the blue mats with our usual jumping jacks. Suddenly, I did an about-face: Wayne and the hockey game vanished from my mind as though wiped out by a tsunami. I stopped my sulking because I had to. If I didn't bring my cold-blooded game face to class, I'd pay for it dearly later.

I was 17 years old, going into my final year of high school, and the "O" had yet to call. The O was the Ontario Hockey League (OHL), the junior league from which "The Show" – the NHL – eventually drafted its players. Sixteen OHL teams had the past two years and a total of 47 rounds to draft me. I should have known they wouldn't since it was the elite triple-A guys they were after. I played for my high school hockey team, the Northern Secondary School Red Knights. We were mostly a patchwork of former single-A and double-A players who now all played for fun. All, that is, except me.

I didn't give up. I continued to play to get noticed. I secretly held out hope that some OHL scout would one day wander into the wrong rink and straight into one of my high school games, during which time he'd witness my Gretzky-esque moves and feel compelled to call his General Manager to tell him he's discovered a hidden gem. I would enter the OHL this way, take the league by storm (*A small skinny kid out of nowhere is tearing up the OHL, would scream one headline in the local newspaper*), get drafted by an NHL team and finally make it to The Show.

Alas, no scout ever wandered into my games, and I was never picked up. It wasn't until one bleary-eyed morning in September that I took a long hard look at myself in my dresser mirror and smelled the kimchi – literally. My mom had probably opened the fridge, and that familiar stench of rotting napa cabbage and salted shrimps was wafting in the air. I wiped the morning guck from my eyes and stood there. It was time. I finally admitted to myself that the OHL wasn't going to be calling. My child-hood dream came crashing down like water from a broken dam in that one moment and, with it, a core chunk of who I was.

I sunk into the spongey cushion of the walnut sofa in our living room, leaned back and, with remote control in hand, began flipping through the channels. It was a frigid Sunday morning in February, and I was content to stay home and veg. *What ever happened to those classic Kung Fu movies with bad dubbing?* I missed them.

I then heard the swooshing of feet along carpet and glanced over to my right to see my mom's small pudgy frame sauntering my way. She plopped down on the cushion next to me.

"How about study in Korea?" she asked me with a noticeable twinkle in her eyes.

I turned to her. What? Study in another country, another culture, another lan-guage? Why? I had already made up my mind to study pre-medicine at McMaster University the next year.

"*Nuh-nun hanguk saram-ee-ya,*" she said, turning very serious. "Your blood Korean, nebuh Canadian."

"Yeah, but …" I didn't have a good rebuttal at the ready.

While I looked the part, I definitely didn't play the part. I spent my whole life in Toronto and, for all intents and purposes, I couldn't speak (let alone read or write) Korean.

"You should know where come prom first," she said. "Then you know yourself, and you lib in Canada, with white Canadian, with conpidence."

"But what would I study?" I said, indulging her just to get her off my back.

She handed me the flimsy rectangular booklet she had been holding in her hands.

"This some English inpormation, what you can study at Seoul National University …"

On the cover was a panoramic shot of the university campus' main buildings, set against mountainous and treed terrain. I leafed through the pages. I stopped at the "College of Humanities" page, and my eyes zoomed in on one major in particular: "Oriental philosophy." For some reason, those two words held my attention longer than any of the others.

My mom's suggestion wasn't a complete surprise. My sisters and I were well-versed in her narrative by this time. My parents never planned to stay that long in Canada when they were invited by Keun Abba, my father's older brother and the pioneer of the Choi clan. He was an engineer who emigrated from South Korea back in the late '60s, and he paved the way for his father, mother, four younger brothers and one sister to follow suit in the early '70s. Keun Abba ended up re-emigrating, to America several years later while the rest of the family stayed in Toronto.

My parents' plan was to stay until they saved enough money to return to the motherland and buy a house. Back then, South Korea was a developing country, still recovering from decades of brutal Japanese occupation (1910-1945), the end of which tore in half the country into the present-day democratic South and communist North, foreshadowed the Korean War (1950-53) that erupted between the two sides only five years later and triggered a military coup d'état in the '60s. Before they knew it, life happened, 20 years had passed, and they were still in Canada.

Although my mom was Canadian on paper, she was Korean at heart. She never let go of her love for her home and native land. She mourned the fact she wasn't able to instill more "Koreanness" into us as we grew up, which was inevitable considering she and my father worked 16-hour days, seven days a week, running Crosstown Discount. In her eyes, my two sisters and I had lost our center and become too Western. We were "bananas" – yellow on the outside, white on the inside. Eastern body, Western mind. She yearned for the day we would discover our cultural roots and become Eastern body, Eastern mind, Western icing on the surface.

Something curious happened. The idea of studying in Korea, as absurd as it seemed, lingered in my head for weeks afterward. The longer it hung around, the less absurd the idea appeared. In fact, it grew on me.

I was Canadian, yes. Well, sort of. Okay, I wasn't sure how much. There was something off about me, maybe for as long as I could remember.

Most of my friends at school looked more like Wayne than I did, which put them in the All-Canadian category and me on the outside peering in. Not many people knew that "Glen" was my Canadian alias; my real name was my Korean one, "Shakwon," until, that is, I pestered my mom to change it. I didn't like hearing the dragged-out nasal whining of my elementary school classmates, who (intentionally) pronounced the "kwon" part as if I was a flying duck that they were hailing to land.

There was also the fact I had to take my shoes off at home, which I didn't realize was a backwards custom until I visited my friend's place after school: "No, dear, no need to take off your shoes," was the common refrain from Ari's chuckling babysitter or Barth's smiling mother.

"Glen, will you be staying for dinner?" Chris' mom said after Chris and I played video games at his house one day. It wasn't long before Chris' home filled with the thick aroma of vegetable soup and grilled meat.

"Say when," Ari's babysitter said to me one evening. Say what? She was grinding the black pepper into my bowl of soup.

"Uh, *when* … ?" I said with absolute uncertainty. The babysitter and Ari burst out laughing.

"You're hilarious!" she said. They thought I was trying to be funny.

Ari's babysitter later brought out large individual plates, at the center of which lay thin slices of roast beef with gravy dripping off the sides, flanked by a mound of mashed potatoes and a sprinkling of salad greens. I fumbled with my cutlery, fork in left hand, knife in the right. Slice, dissect, transfer to mouth, I had to remind myself. Everything seemed so square in shape – neat, tidy and contained.

The dining table at our house felt like a bustling Chinatown in comparison. Our spread featured exotic Korean sauces, spices and pastes. There were bowls of sticky white rice, one for each of us, and several small plates of pickled vegetables, sesame-oil seasoned bean sprouts and roasted seaweed or anchovies at the center of the table, all of which we nipped at with our metal chopsticks. At the center of these side dishes, the center of our dining universe, sat a large steaming pot of miso stew or sometimes kimchi or spicy cod stew, which soon became a free-for-all in double-dipping.

Many of my current classmates at Northern hung out with their girlfriends/boyfriends after school. Meanwhile, I would make a beeline for Northern District Public Library because I was expected to get straight A's and go to the University of Toronto. My parents believed that the romantic syrupy stuff was silly and unable to fulfill long-term well-being requirements. It was something that would work itself out in the end anyway, after we graduated from a top university and found a nice career.

Not that much would have changed had I been allowed to socialize more. I wasn't very good at small talk. I only spoke to my high school classmates when it was absolutely necessary, and "How's it going?" or "What's new with you?" never felt absolutely necessary. So I clung to Barth – my one holdover friend from my elementary school days – and a few Chinese and Vietnamese friends, with whom I could avoid the small talk and discuss only serious matters, like school work and our marks. They got me, and me them.

At lunchtime, I would descend to the bowels of the school building, the basement floor, where I ate in the cafeteria with the gang. Some of us walked over to the adjacent library afterward. There we would chat in whispers while sitting on the carpeted floor in a far corner. I often stole glances at the ceiling as we did, imagining hundreds of Northerners outside, gabbing, laughing and flirting away their youth, lovesick couples staring deep into each other's eyes. The only time girls looked at me was when I was in their way.

Maybe that's it, I thought.

I began to question whether I was more Korean than Canadian, and I just didn't know it. Maybe there was something to the blood thing. Perhaps I was genetically wired like native Koreans, that is, to be more serious and reserved? It would explain a lot. Besides hockey, I didn't really fit in in Canada. Was I, then, trying to deny a part of me that was, as my mom put it, undeniable? Maybe I'd feel more whole and confident if I went over to the yellow side?

Over the next few days, I shifted my thoughts to distant memories, memories of visits to the local Korean Buddhist temple growing up: the glistening bald heads, humble grey robes and calming demeanor of the Korean monks; the unusual yet enchanting scent of incense wafting in the air; the life-sized gilt statue of the Buddha at the center of the main hall; the grounding and centering experience of sitting on a mat cross-legged; the strange and mystical sounds of monks chanting; and the fresh vegetarian fare that was made with love and served once the service ended.

Korea began to mushroom in my mind as a land shrouded in the mysteries and mysticism of the Orient. I then envisioned an epic journey about to unfold in my life:

24

I travel to one of the heartlands of Oriental philosophy.

There, I spend long days, months and years at Seoul National University, engrossed in the study of something profound and mystical, taught by the elite of the elite in the field.

Content and confident with the base of knowledge and wisdom I've accumulated, I eventually return to Canada, where I breeze through graduate school. It isn't long before the University of Toronto comes calling to teach.

Now alone in my office, I sit in my reclining leather chair, one leg crossed over the other. I am wearing a navy blue cardigan and puffing on my pipe. Thick curls of smoke meander their way

through the shelves of books and up to the ceiling lights.

I gently tug on the lush strands of salt-and-pepper hair on my chin as I peer out the window. I marvel at the sea of ivy growing up and along the campus buildings.

I then turn my gaze inward and bask in the knowledge of hard-earned triumphs: not only have I become a much sought-after scholar of Oriental philosophy, whose penetrating insights have captured the imagination of my colleagues worldwide; on a personal level I have truly reconciled the "Korean" and "Canadian" sides of me.

Eureka. I found my calling in life, my passion project, and I felt nourished because I belonged once again, this time to the esteemed pantheon of wise Oriental philosophers. Becoming a medical doctor never seemed quite as cool after that.

I announced my future plans to my father the next day. As the patriarch of the family, he had to give the final stamp of approval.

"Oh, *gurae?*" he said as he put down the Korean community newspaper he was reading on the sofa and let out a few hearty ho-ho-ho's. His laughter was pregnant with pride. "Omma told me already."

He paused for a moment and then leaned over. "*Ung, gureo-kuna* ... Seoul National University? That is best in Korea. Same like Harvard in Korea. Don't worry money, just concentrate on study. I support you 100 percent."

I wasn't looking forward to saying bye to Barth, my best buddy at Northern and, really, since Allenby Elementary School. I'd especially miss our competitions to one-up each other, whether through better grades in school or in whatever sport we played – tennis, one-on-one baseball, ping pong or shinny hockey. In fact, I imagined it would be so painful to tell him that I revealed only half the truth.

"I'm going to Korea for the summer," I blurted to Barth one day as we trotted home from school with knapsacks slung over our shoulders.

Barth stopped dead in his tracks and turned to me.

"What?" he said. "*When* in the summer? And *why?*" I could see the muscles around his chiseled jawline tighten. With his dirty brown hair, scrawny build and the beat-up T-shirt he had on, he kind of looked like Kurt Cobain and lost.

"To learn Korean. I'm going to learn at a language institute there, for most of the summer ..." I braced myself for the fury of objections that he would unleash.

"But Glen ..." he said in a plaintive whisper. He was too indignant to emote properly.

I didn't want to hold up pedestrian traffic, so I motioned to him to keep walking.

"We had so much planned for this summer, our last before uni. Tennis, road hockey, baseball, Burger Shack ..."

"I know, but ..."

Good ol' Burger Shack. He knew how to tug on my heartstrings. Some of my fondest memories were the post-shinny hockey meals we shared at Burger Shack in the winters: with our noses running and hands quivering, Barth and I would bite into our fat juicy banquet burgers, and we both knew, in that moment at least, there was nothing more satisfying in the world.

But the good times I had with Barth – and the many more that could have come – were no match for the visions of greatness dancing in my head. When I was passionate about an idea, I went full force ahead with blinders on.

4
Fiery Baptism

"THAT'S AWESOME!
@#$%&@#&@#$%& … This semester's going to be fun! @#$%&@#$%&@%&
… Oh my! @#$%&@#$%&@#$%& …"

Oh my was right. Other than picking up the odd interjection, I was drowning in a sea of Korean chatter of more than 30 freshmen and women. Twenty percent of what I was hearing was Korean; the rest was Greek to me. Was it Shakespeare who wrote that life is full of sound and fury, signifying nothing?

I muted the noise and stared out the bus window. It was still half-coated with morning frost.

How did I get here, again?

It seemed like only yesterday I was back in Sweet Home Toronto, a student at Northern Secondary, where the hallways filled with the music of the English language and multiple colorful streaks of white, black and yellow skin. Encasing the hallways were the classrooms where I shared, with some, my dreams about studying the ways of the mystical Far East.

Fast forward 10 months and poof! I was now on a chartered bus bustling with *English* majors from Seoul National University, heading to a mountain retreat center east of Seoul for Orientation, or Frosh Week as it was known in Canada. Surrounding me were people with straight jet-black hair and black eyes. Period. I was living an episode of Star Trek, in an alternate universe amongst a race of people who were clones … of me. Fiction had become reality and my old reality like fiction.

Eyes on the prize, I quickly reminded myself, steadying my gaze through the window.

I had a Master Plan. I would study in the English department at SNU for the first two years, as a sort of language buffer zone before switching over to Oriental philosophy. Indeed, what I was hearing on the bus only confirmed my earlier suspicions: the six months of level-5 and -6 language classes I recently passed would not be enough to understand Korean-language lectures, let alone read Buddhist tomes.

We arrived at the retreat center a couple of hours later, that is, our bus and an endless parade of other chartered buses carrying about 600 frosh from the different departments in the College of Humanities. Koreans put the "C" in collectively when they party, I thought. In his most recent handwritten letter to me, Barth had mentioned that Frosh Week at the University of Toronto only involved a hundred or so frosh from his college unit. (He added that he hoped I would come to my senses and return to Toronto immediately.)

The air was refreshing and February crisp when I got off the bus. I inhaled deeply, and the cold air tickled my nose hairs. *Ah, nice.* A tall red-brick building stood above several lodge-type structures strewn along a strip of flat land. In the backdrop were rolling mountains that, from afar, looked as if they were covered in green mold. I couldn't remember the last time I saw such vast and open space, if ever.

We grabbed our bags from the bus and scurried to our designated lodge, weaving our way through the throngs of students and the scene of anarchy that lay before us. We followed the lead of a few sophomore students from our department. The sophomores didn't have a name. Well, they did, but I couldn't remember them because I had to address them as *sunbae*, or "senior classmate." It reminded me of my older sister, whom I had to address as Nuna, or "older sister," rather than by her first name, Heesun. (Much to the chagrin of my mom, I started to call my older sister "Nunes" in high school because the extra syllable was annoying.) Koreans, I figured, believed older individuals had more life experiences and were therefore wiser and more knowledgeable than the younger folk. They played the role of invaluable mentor to the next generation. So treating such individuals as equals by, for example, calling them by their first name was considered disrespectful.

Once inside, we dropped our bags in the corners and were instructed to sit on the floor in a circle. The air in the room was dull and chilly, so I kept my jacket on. I sat down where I was, cross-legged, although my tight jeans did their best to resist. I lowered my gaze and waited in silence, pressing the tips of my entwined fingers hard against my knuckles. I stole furtive glances around the room. About half of my department was women. I squirmed and swayed my upper body and re-crossed my legs. I then spread them forward, bent my knees and wrapped my arms around them. My legs weren't used to sitting cross-legged for an extended length of time.

The trio of *sunbaes*, who remained standing, spoke up. They introduced themselves one by one. I forgot their names just as soon as the next person started speaking. Korean names didn't register in my head the way English ones did, in part because Korean nomenclature started with the surname, which threw me off. I was "Choi Glen" here, not "Glen Choi," and my identity was literally reversed in my new world.

My classmates woo-hooed and clapped after their intros.

"Now," one of the male *sunbaes* said, "we'd like each of you to stand up, one by one, and introduce yourselves."

I felt a sharp pain in the pit of my stomach. I had never given a speech in front of native Koreans before, let alone in their own language. Come to think of it, I had rarely done this in English.

The introductions started at one end of the circle. Luckily, I was sitting in the middle of the pack, which gave me the much-needed time to formulate in my head how to say what I wanted to say.

The first person got up to speak. It was game on, and my heart started pounding. Korean verbs, nouns, articles, connectors, conjugations: these were all jumbled and floating around in my brain, and I had to quickly catch them, bring them down, arrange them in order and then rehearse in my head at least once before I opened my mouth. I felt like a rookie stand-up comedian about to test his material in front of a live audience.

Shoot. The first two people who spoke didn't just say hi and state their names for the record. I was hoping they would because that, then, would be the general expectation of me. They said hi, my name is so-and-so, and – I couldn't believe it – touched on their motivations for studying English. They then ended with some obligatory rhetoric: "I look forward to getting to know all of you better during Orientation."

I should do the same, I told myself. *You don't want to be seen as the aloof, non-conformist type, Glen.*

The English version of my spiel was done in my head in 30 seconds:

> Hi, my name is Glen Choi, and I'm from Canada. I want to study Oriental philosophy later on, but I chose English literature for now because my Korean language skills still need work. I look forward to getting to know all of you better during Orientation.

Perfect. I immediately went to work on translating this into Korean.

Shit. How do you say "for now" again? I thought. My brain felt constipated. I pushed and pushed until the word popped out.

Right, "*imshi*."

And "still need work"? I think "*bujok hada*"?

I had to get English syntax out of my head. No, I told myself, it was no longer subject-verb-object, but subject-*object*-verb. My brain felt murky as I made the switch, as if I was swimming upstream through a polluted river.

As my turn to speak inched ever closer, the mental chatter devolved into a frenzied pitch.

> *Deep breath.*
> *What if I blank?*
> *Shush.*
> *How many more people 'til my turn?*

My turn had arrived. The world unfolded before me in a dreamy slo-mo sequence.

The time it took me to pick myself up off the floor, stand up, give my shirt a quick tug and clear my throat seemed like minutes rather than seconds. Once I opened my mouth, my brain made a sharp right turn onto a highway and picked up speed. I completed my speech in what seemed like a few seconds, when it was probably closer to a minute in reality.

As I sat back down to a round of obligatory applause, the stiffness in my neck, arms and legs began to loosen. The ordeal was over, and my anxiety dissolved into a quiet sigh. I could now sit back, relax and enjoy the rest of the show. But my mind made a sharp U-ey. It demanded I conduct a post-mortem analysis of my spiel: was the grammar perfect? Did I say anything awkward? Did I embarrass myself … ?

"*Sarang haeyo.*"

Out of the corner of my ear did I hear this. It was said in the soft gooey lilt of a mother fawning over her 2-month-old baby. The hairs on the back of my neck stood on end. Neither I nor any of my friends from Northern – female or male – ever talked like that to each other. This was an attempt at cuteness, obviously, but it was overkill, cringeworthy, beyond normal, at least for the situation. Yet I heard only a round of warm chuckles and impassioned applause from the audience afterward. I looked up to my left to see a blushing female classmate sitting back down.

Wait a minute, I thought – something else is funny here. *Sarang haeyo* just means "to love," the verb only. Did I miss something? Love whom? And who loves whom?

Once the introductions were complete and our group dispersed, I meandered my way over to Hae-il, a tall and lanky classmate to whom I gravitated on the bus ride over. He spoke in soft and inviting monotones. I asked him what our classmate meant by *sarang haeyo*.

"You don't know the meaning of '*Sarang hae*?'" he said, somewhat surprised.

"I do," I said. "But … she loves somebody … ?"

He chuckled. "She loves all of us, her classmates," he said as he pushed his thick black-rimmed glasses up his nose.

"But I didn't hear 'I' and 'all of you.'"

"You don't need it, because it's implied."

"Oh … right …"

It did sound familiar. Did I learn this in Korean class? I remembered something about shortcuts like this. The "I" was often omitted in sentences. "Went to school," Koreans would say, rather than "I went to school." I figured this was because the "I" was obvious in these utterances and therefore redundant.

Afterwards, our group made our way to the larger main building to have lunch in the cafeteria. For some reason, what my female classmate said earlier stuck in my head like a bug in my ear. I thought about her remark in between spoonfuls of steamed rice and seasoned vegetables. I thought about it when we walked back to our lodge and unpacked.

"Love" – not "I love you."

I was certainly not in love with her; I only met her today. No, it wasn't that … Her remark felt breezy and naked. I liked the focus on the verb, the act, on continuous movement, on flow.

Yes, yes.

"I" and "you" were these big, bulky and immobile walls that only served to ground the action, the movement, to a halt. They dammed up flowing water on either side. And when river water stops moving, it suffocates and stagnates. Removing the dams "I" and "you" released "love" from its imprisonment, and it was allowed to breathe and flow again.

Aha. I liked it because it felt freeing!

Either that or I was being melodramatic. They were, after all, just words. How could mere words set me free? Whatever the case, the mental chatter stopped after this little insight, and I won back my peace of mind.

The sun was sparkling the next morning. A chilly breeze dulled the air and frosted the morning dew that glistened atop the picnic tables. Several of my classmates and I hopped around on our left leg along the gravel-strewn paths nearby. I eyeballed my opponents from our rival French department, hunched over and primed to knock down whoever came my way, my folded and jutting right knee my weapon.

Bam! *Yes!* I just felled one of their guys.

I might have been small, but they didn't know who they were up against. Well, a tough Canadian boy who used to play hockey, that's who. Moments later, I made eye contact with a guy from the opposing team who made a beeline for me. He stopped in front of me, then leaped to slam his knee down on my thigh, and I slipped, leaving me with gravel imprints on the palm of my right hand. I was eliminated from the game.

I wasn't given much time to lick my wounds. Our group returned to the lodge to play another game. We sat on the floor in a circle and slowly started clapping our hands and slapping our laps in rhythm, then quickened the pace, until the rhythm escalated into a heart-pounding tribal beat.

Slap, clap, slap, clap –

"Choi, Glen," a male classmate from the far end of the circle shouted. *Me, already?*

I had to call out another classmate's name without breaking rhythm.

"Lee … uhh …"

I was eliminated. I sat hunched over as I watched the rest of the game play itself out. The tribal beat continued, only this time we had to calculate numbers on the spot.

Slap, clap –

"1 and 2 …"

"3 and 4 …"

"7 and 8 …"

"15 and 16 …"

Me: "17 and 18 …"

"Aaayyy," my classmates said in unison, giving voice to their mental finger-wagging.

After lunch, our department moved to one of the smaller rooms inside the main building, where we broke off into cells of five to 10 people. We again sat on the floor in circles. I preferred this room over our lodge because it was sheeted with *jangpan-ji*, a thick malleable layer of moon-yellow oiled paper that molded to my jutting ankle bones. It was also warm because it was *ondol*, the radiant underfloor heating typical of traditional Korean homes. The floor of our lodge was cement-hard, a lacquered white, and cold.

My cell-group mates proceeded to rattle off sentences in machine-gun succession. They also threw out one subject matter after another like someone madly rummaging through a chest of old clothes. *Uh-oh*. I felt like I was back on the bus that first day coming over.

What I was hearing didn't sound like the Korean I learned in language class. This new Korean seemed much softer around the edges, less clearly enunciated and full of grammatical shortcuts. I imagined a ragbag of slang, idioms and cultural references that I never learned were thrown in for good measure. Welcome to the world of "real Korean," I said in my head with a wry smile.

I played the role of Silent Bob the whole time, nodding my head every now and then in feigned agreement. But I yearned to contribute to the discussion so I could feel part of the gang. That's it; I'm going to say something no matter what, I told myself.

I bore down and hyper-focused. First order of business: grasp the current topic of discussion.

Okay. My classmates are talking about forming study groups in the upcoming semester.

Aha. This was an easy one as far as what I should say. I would express my interest in joining and offer my help in any way as a native English speaker. This was ingenious. I would be seen as someone who offered value to the group, and they would, in return, embrace me. I tuned out the others as I jumbled together a couple of Korean sentences in my head.

Okay, sentences done.

They probably weren't grammatically pristine, but they'd have to do. So long as I got my message across.

When I was ready to speak, I pointed my index finger skyward, furrowed my eyebrows and pursed my lips. One by one, my classmates peripherally caught sight of this amidst the current ongoing discussion. When the person speaking began winding down her talk and her last word dropped off into an ellipsis, they all turned to face me with a look of great anticipation. I hardly ever spoke, and they genuinely wanted to hear from me.

"I think study groups are a good idea. I would like to help. Maybe I can help with English words that you don't know."

I did it.

I immediately felt better about myself and my standing in the group because I contributed something of value to them.

Or what I thought was something of value.

My comment was followed by a moment of awkward silence. The rest of the group turned their gazes up or downward, to the right or left, any way to avoid eye contact with me.

"Thank you, Glen," my female *sunbae* said, finally breaking the silence. "That sounds like a wonderful idea … That's right; we were talking about that a little while ago."

She then slowly turned to face the rest of the group. "So as we were saying …"

Back at the lodge, the beer and soju (rice liquor) started flowing in the evening, and the subsequent parlor games soon transformed into the trading floor of the New York Stock Exchange – animated bodies and boisterous voices clamoring for attention from every direction.

Sigh.

Alas, there was never any alone-time, no time to breathe, no rest for the weary, and by "weary" I meant only me. My classmates clapped, bantered, laughed, sang, jeered and cheered more loudly in the wee hours than in the early afternoon. They were quiet bespectacled bookworms by day, frat boys and girls by night.

I could only behold the spectacle as I chewed on ripped strands of roasted squid and downed a paper cup filled with Korean lager. Until this week, I never enjoyed the bitterness of beer or the lighter-fluidness of soju, but peer pressure and the onslaught of the stress from having to express myself in a foreign language fixed that in a matter of days.

I'm witnessing the tsunami of years of pent-up energies, I observed. I saw this coming when I stayed at my uncle's house for a month after I first arrived in Seoul. My high school-aged cousins went to school by 8 a.m. and typically returned home at 10 p.m., after all the homework, individual tutoring and music lessons (usually piano) were done. This was a typical school day for *all* high school students in Korea, a routine that ran for three straight years. The competition to get into one of only a handful of elite universities in the capital city of Seoul was fierce and cutthroat.

My parents also demanded academic excellence and that my sisters learn the piano and I the violin (and later some guitar). But we sometimes played sports after school, were usually home before supper, and got to watch our favorite TV shows in the evening. We actually had a *life*. There was no comparison.

I received some particularly grim news on the third night. The Frosh Week organizing committee announced that each department would be required to perform a skit on stage in front of the rest of the hundreds of Humanities students in two days, at the end of Orientation.

After dinner, our department gathered again in the smaller room to decide on a premise for our skit, which, from what I could make out, was a story about a husband, his wife and their children. As I sat there in the meeting, it dawned on me that I had nothing to worry about. My classmates would never be so cruel as to ask a foreign student who couldn't speak the language to play any substantial role in the skit. I'd probably be asked to play an extra in the background, some pedestrian passerby in a busy street scene.

Several minutes later, the mile-a-minute chatter died down, and all 30-plus eyeballs turned to me. I was a deer in headlights. The world, once again, unfolded before me in slow motion. One of my *sunbaes* turned to me one small jerking motion at a time, and the words that came out of his mouth plodded forth, slurred, obnoxiously loud, like a drunk person speaking through a megaphone:

"YYYOOOUUU … LEAD actor."

My heart dropped, and my face grew pale.

> *What? Are you all out of your collective gourds?*
> *Let me get this straight: it's not enough that I'm torturing myself trying to formulate one meager sentence in Korean?*
> *We need to amp up the suffering by forcing me to say multiple sentences on multiple topics throughout multiple scenes in front of 600 of my peers – is that the idea?*

That's what I wanted to say, if I had the guts to. But I was still feeling fragile and on the cusp of unravelling like a delicately wrapped sushi roll because the stressors weren't letting up. I felt compelled to say *something*, even if I had no time to think about how I was going to say it and thereby butcher the Korean language (not to mention my pride) in the process.

I tried to stay as calm and composed as possible under the circumstances.

"Uhh …" I said in a trembling voice, "since I can't speak Korean very well, I don't think …"

My *sunbae* quickly raised his long gangly right arm as if to object, then gently placed his bony fingers on my shoulder and leaned over.

"No, no. You don't have to say anything."

"Really? But how … ?"

"You just need to act with your body."

I discovered there would be no dialogue on anyone's part because the lead and supporting cast would be pantomiming the whole time. Meanwhile, those without a role would be singing a chorus in the background.

A number of my classmates chimed in at once to tell me they thought I would make a great lead actor. *What am I going to do, say no?* I didn't want to develop a reputation as being lame and a party-pooper, especially since I was already on the fringes of the mainstream. I relented and agreed to play the lead. I wasn't entirely off the hook, though. I would have to listen for cues from the skit's narrator to follow the plot and know when to pantomime what. The thought of this alone made my heart sink because I didn't want to screw up in front of hundreds of people.

I discovered the lead role I would be playing was the wife. Yep, it just kept getting better and better. My classmates wanted the "right" man to play it for comedic effect and, apparently, out of all the men in our department, they thought I looked the most effeminate.

For our first rehearsal the next afternoon, I was asked to wrap and tie a white towel around my head, wear the red lipstick graciously provided by one of my female classmates, and slip on a plump plaid dress to wear over my jeans. As my classmates stole grinning glances at me, I detected a peculiar pattern. The constant "public speaking," the group games, and now this skit in front of hundreds of people. This couldn't have been a coincidence. I was my unlucky classmate on our first day of school at Glenview, my junior high school, who was dragged down the grassy hill of the schoolyard on his butt by the older 8th grade kids. He had to walk around school all day with grass burn on his spanking new back-to-school black leather pants. Of course, this wasn't as blatant and childish as that. And it wasn't just one person, that is, me. We were all being constantly poked, prodded and ribbed by our *sunbae*, although my classmates appeared to handle it better than I did, probably because they spoke the language fluently.

I then felt an odd emotion. It was the spark of excitement. My heart seemed to relish the experience. I did my best to ignore it – my ego was telling me a different story. But it was too strong to deny. I had always felt trapped inside the cavity of my own skull, reserved, as though I wasn't meant to stand out. Every time I stood up to address my classmates and risk embarrassment, I kicked at the steely bars and put a good dent in them. With each kick, I was creating more wiggle room to break free from some of my most intense fears, from inhibition. I felt vulnerable, yes, but alive.

I also felt a special bond with my classmates in such moments. My risk was paid in kind. "I'll risk my ego if you risk yours," was our tacit agreement. Even if it was somewhat easier for them, we were in this together. We were being vulnerable together, even if I felt more so. Could this be the reason we were all being subject to such torture? These "naked" moments might coax us to lower our guards, to chip away at the stone walls with which we protected our individual egos, and to open ourselves up to each other and the world. That, in turn, would build trust between us and strengthen our bonds. Koreans had a word for this – *jung*. It was one of the first cultural concepts I learned in language school. There is no single equivalent bon mot for it in English. *Jung* is like the word "affection," only stronger and deeper. It refers to the familial love and trust you develop with non-family members, such as friends, colleagues, co-workers, through the many shared good times and bad, in much the same way a person grows to love someone "like a brother or sister."

Was the end purpose of all this, then, simply one big exercise in building group trust and solidarity? If it was, I just couldn't understand why it was so important to do so to the extent that we did for an academic department. For sports teams or the military, yes, because the competition is unforgiving and winning is everything. But for an academic department within the university, let alone the university itself? There was no championship or battle to be won in the end, as far as I could tell.

Lights out. I slumped to the floor, zipped up my black sleeping bag and laid my head on my folded T-shirt for a pillow. The deafening sounds of drunken merriment from the evening had died down. My ears, however, were still ringing. My classmates and *sunbaes* nestled into their sleeping bags, which littered the floor. Almost immediately, I heard snoring coming from the far corner. I laid there and looked up into the utter blackness of the air. Without so much as a silent minute to hear myself think during the day, bedtime was the one window through which I could escape to a warmer climate.

My mind drifted to the good times I had living in Toronto. I missed my room, my bed, my pillow, spending long lazy days at home on Sundays and playing shinny hockey with Barth or my cousins John and Peter at Eglinton Park. I missed the home-made banquet burger at Burger Shack. I reminisced about my past crushes and the experiences of requited and unrequited love – dating back to Joanne and Jessica in elementary school. I also missed speaking English with Nunes at our Homestay room in Seoul, even though I had only been away from her for a few days. Thank god, I thought, that finishing up her biology degree at Yonsei University in Seoul was just the "adventure" Nunes was seeking in her life at the time. It was reassuring to know that my big sis – who was taller than me and tomboy tough – had my back over here. Even though it was only February, I couldn't wait for next Christmas when I would go home to visit Toronto.

I then questioned my decision to study in Korea in earnest for the first time. It looked like I had badly miscalculated.

> *Why didn't you think this through more, Glen?*
> *You could've been breezing through life in Canada right now.*
> *You might look the part, but you're more Canadian than you think.*

Just as soon as I started to feel sorry for myself, however, another voice bullied its way to the forefront of my head, leaving broken shards of china in its wake. It was the voice of my father.

> *So what?*
> *Why you so afraid of ko-nuh!?*

I snapped out of my self-pitying and to attention. I transformed into a different person. It was me in Mr. Lee's judo class. It was me for the following two years playing hockey where, with thinking changed, the game mutated from art form to war zone, opposing players from teens decked out in colorful team outfits to the cloned storm-troopers of the Galactic Empire: their helmets glinted an unfeeling metal, their pupils were black and beady and their expressions steely and cemented. They were dark and sinister alien beings, and they had to be destroyed. Come game time, my focus turned laser-like, and I became hyper-present, my sole mission to seek and destroy. I had done the same just now. The growing mental chatter and voices of self-pity cowered in the wake of my hyper-present focus and soon dissipated. I also soon fell fast asleep.

Skit day arrived. In the hours before show time, the pressure and anxiety continued to mount. The idea that 600 pairs of eyeballs would be fixed on me and my every move during the performance grew closer to becoming reality. I was able to live a relatively safe and low-profile life in Canada for the past 18 years, but I had been living on borrowed time. This time there was nowhere to hide from the spotlight.

My classmates and I rose from our seats in the auditorium and marched together in procession backstage. We were due up next. I heard the thunderous applause of the audience followed by the muffled words of the MC, and my heart started pounding. The current skit was over, and the moment of truth had arrived. We ascended the stairs and took our places on stage.

The curtains drew to the sides, and the stage lights blinded my eyes. In that moment, I felt a heightened sense of awareness and concentration. Out of nowhere, perhaps desperate for a spark of inspiration to live up to the demands of my 600 peers in the audience, my mind latched onto the image of Las Vegas showgirls I had seen on TV over the years. I immediately changed my hitherto straight and stiff stance and bent my right leg out to the side, tilted my head up to the sky and put one hand behind my head.

Roars of laughter.

They like it. Go with it, Glen.

And so I did. I ran with it. Then one hiccup. At the midway point, my "husband" leapfrogged over me after I bent over, as per the rehearsals. Unlike in the rehearsals, he accidentally knocked the towel off my head as he leapt. I didn't flinch. I dropped to my knees, crawled forward and plopped the still-intact wig back on as though nothing had happened. More laughter.

At the closing ceremony that evening, I was called to the stage by the MC – I had won the Most Popular Actor award. For my efforts, I received a roll of flipchart paper. When I returned to my seat, I was greeted with a round of "congratulations!" and high-fives from my classmates and *sunbaes*. The rush of adrenaline coursed through my veins unabated as the awards continued.

And continued.

And continued some more.

By this time, only the embers of the adrenaline remained, and I began to intermittently glance up at the clock. I suspected the judging committee wanted to ensure no department went home empty-handed so that no one felt left out. When the ceremony ended and people rose from their seats, I looked down at the flipchart paper I was cradling in my arms. It had lost some of the white luster that I saw when I first went up to receive it.

We returned to our lodges to freshen up for dinner. My hands were still trembling from the buzz I got from performing. The pressure – the rush of adrenaline – the heightened awareness – the unleashing of creative energy – the ability to think and act on my feet – the roar of laughter and applause from the audience: this was all intoxicating stuff.

I lined up in the communal cafeteria with my steel food tray in hand. The kitchen staff plopped various foods into the appropriate tray compartments as I moved along the serving counter. I walked over to our department table.

"Glen, *hwa-ee-ting*!" one of my female classmates said to me as I sat down next to her. I remembered learning that word, probably on the bus ride over. *Hwa-ee-ting* was the Korean phoneticized version of the English word "fighting," which somehow evolved in the Korean language to mean something like "good job!" (among other meanings, depending on the circumstances).

"Thanks," I said.

I looked across the table from me to see a couple of my male classmates nod their heads my way, with a smile. I blushed and smiled back. The attention was embarrassing and unwanted. Okay, not entirely. It did feel good to be popular, for once.

Our table turned quiet. Everybody was hungry and busy chowing down. I picked up my metal chopsticks and transferred bits of food from this and that tray compartment into my mouth. I stared straight ahead as I munched on a savory mix of moist white rice, kimchi and *bulgogi* – thin slices of grilled beef marinated in sesame oil and soy sauce, among other spices. My mind returned to the events that had just transpired. I realized that pressure and stress could actually be beneficial. It not only made me feel alive, it pushed me to rise to the occasion and perform, the reward for which was hundreds of people approving and applauding.

5

The Alpha Male

"PARDON ME FOR ASKING," JAE-IL HYUNG said to the five of us, "but what religion are all of you?"

I was in a dimly lit basement café in the Shinchon neighborhood with two of my male classmates and three female frosh students from Ewha Women's University. We were on a three-on-three blind date.

"I'm Catholic," said one of the female students.

"I'm Christian," said another.

"I'm Christian, too," said the third.

Then it was the guys' turn.

"I'm Christian," said Jae-il hyung. I had to add the suffix *hyung*, literally meaning "older brother," to Jae-il's name because he was a year older than me.

"I'm also Christian," said Jeong-su hyung, my other older SNU classmate who had joined us.

I hesitated for a moment before chiming in – I realized I was about to become the black sheep of the bunch.

"I'm Buddhist," I said.

Everyone laughed.

"How ironic," said Jae-il hyung, grinning, "that all of us follow Christianity except for Glen, the lone Westerner here."

Chuckles and murmurs of agreement.

There was something very familiar about our group tonight. It then occurred to me. In the faces of the young men and women at the table here did I see my cousins' reflections. Followed by flickering images of the rest of the Choi clan back home in Toronto, my uncles and aunts, who were all Christian. Protestant, mostly. Most of the Koreans I knew in Toronto were Christian. The times, as Bob Dylan crooned, were certainly a changin', and I was fast becoming an anachronism, a fossil dug up within the graves of the Korean religious landscape. The proof of my minority status was everywhere around me. In fact, I had lived a double minority's life in Canada, ethnically as a Korean in Toronto and religiously as a Buddhist within the local Korean community. And in Korea, where I presumed Buddhists dominated the religious demographic, I was still a double minority, as a Westerner and a Buddhist, at least within our own group tonight. I had become a double-double minority.

We chatted some more. I sat there nursing a glass of Coke with a bopping yellow straw inside, a vacuous smile marking my face. I wasn't any better than before at keeping up with the rapid-fire back-and-forth and the fleetingness of subject matter, not to mention deciphering the poorly enunciated words. But dammit I was going to contribute because I was very jealous: as far as I could tell, Jae-il and Jeong-su hyung were charming the ladies with their wit and humor.

"I know a joke," I blurted.

My lips froze and pupils darted left and right, as though I had just farted and was hoping no one noticed. But everyone heard. They all turned to look at me. My brain's safety switch just blew a fuse, and there was no turning back now. I had dived into the deep end when I wasn't even a good swimmer. I had no time to rehearse in my head how I was going to frame the joke in Korean.

"Well, uhh … why can't Koreans play hockey?" I asked.

This was a joke I heard back in my hockey playing days, as locker-room ribbing from my teammates, and actually the only joke I knew.

"Hockey? Do you mean field hockey?" Jeong-su hyung asked.

"No, ice hockey," I said. "I'm from Canada … so … I meant ice hockey."

"Right," one of the female students said, "I heard that ice hockey was popular in Canada."

"Okay, so why can't Koreans play hockey?" Jae-il hyung anxiously asked.

"Because every time they go into the …"

I blanked on the Korean word for "corner."

"Uhh …" I started to gesture with my hands to visually represent what I meant by the "corner" of an ice rink.

They finally got it.

"It's *ko-nuh* in Korean, too," Jeong-su hyung said with a chuckle.

Apparently, the Korean language had borrowed many English words but pronounced them using their own phonemes.

"Oh, okay. So every time they go into the *ko-nuh*, they open up a variety store," I said.

Crickets.

I knew they were missing the frame of reference to get the joke, but I was in such a rush to impress the ladies I didn't have time to preface it.

"You probably don't know this but, in Canada, most Koreans work in variety stores. On street *ko-nuhs*."

Murmurs of "okay" and "yes …"

"So there's the *ko-nuh* of an ice rink, and the street ko-nuhs where there are variety stores. So when Korean hockey players go into the *ko-nuh* of a rink, they will open up a store and be unable to continue participating in the game …"

I was drowning in my own explanation. I had just mangled all of the key components of a good joke – the set-up, the punchline and the timing and delivery. Not to mention the joke's cultural applicability.

"Oh, I get it, I get it," Jae-il hyung suddenly said.

He turned to the others to explain the joke in crisp clean Korean prose. The "ohhh's" and "I see's" mercifully emerged one by one. There was a god, after all, and he was sitting right next to me.

"Glen, it's better if you refrain from the lame jokes," Jae-il hyung said with a smile.

Everyone laughed, although probably at me and not with me. But I'd take it. I was just relieved to come out the other side, with the bonus of some laughter I had produced in the group, however awkwardly.

After some more chatting, we got down to the nitty-gritty.

"Pick a straw, any straw," said Jae-il hyung, who was the oldest among us and thus the de facto leader.

The three women reached for one of the three differently colored straws that Jae-il hyung had cut in half and placed in a cup.

It was now the guys' turn. Each of us picked the other half of the different-colored straws from the cup, without knowing which color our female counterparts had selected. Matching colored straws determined who your one-on-one date for the evening was.

Damn.

I was really hoping to be paired with the girl at the far end of the table from me, the one with sharp facial features and straight black hair that fell down to her shoulder blades. With her glasses on, she looked both smart and sexy. My date was a little plumper with an oval face and shoulder-length hair. But her skin, which was Snow White pale and flawless, was striking.

"What would you like to eat?" I asked my date as we walked out of the café. I was relieved I was slightly taller than her, even with her high heels on.

"I am not sure," she said softly. "I am quite flexible …"

I had no idea where we could go. What I *did* know was that, in Korea, the guy was supposed to take the lead. I would have to perform again, to play a new role, but this time as the alpha male.

We walked a good 20 minutes before I finally found something.

"How about this one?" I pointed to a small restaurant that looked like it suited our needs – classy-looking yet probably affordable for someone on a student budget.

"Certainly," she said.

We settled into our chairs and looked at the menu.

"I'm going to order the kimchi fried rice," I said soon after. I felt the pressure to decide first. "That's one of my favorite dishes."

"Oh, really?" she said. "I think I will order the same."

As if on cue, our waitress came by to take our orders.

"We will have two kimchi fried rice's," I announced in as deep and authoritative a voice as I could muster.

"Anything to drink?" the waitress said as she took back our menus.

"Just water, thank you," I said, eyeing my date in case she objected.

I leaned forward and crossed my fingers on top of the table.

"Umm, you can drop the formal speech, since we're about the same age, and we've gotten to know each other a little ..."

I was repeating what my frustrated SNU classmates would constantly remind me: "We're the same age and friends now, so you can drop the honorifics!" Korean formal speech was reserved for people who were older than me or whom I was meeting for the first time.

"Yes, in due time, I will ..." my date said, averting her eyes. She was right. We were meeting for the first time and weren't exactly what you'd call friends yet.

"Okay, sure. So how do you like school?"

I steered our conversations to the topics of school, family and future career plans. I could articulate my thoughts on these in Korean without stuttering; they were the questions I was asked most over the past year and, with that much practice, now my go-to talking points. This well inevitably dried up, though, at which time I brought up whatever topic came to mind and mobilized every grammatical pattern I could remember. I wanted to keep the conversation moving forward. Every moment of awkward silence was, to me, a moment of beta weakness.

We finished our meals and, after some more conversation, I paid our waitress, and we got up to leave. We stood outside the restaurant. I waited until the last moment to ask for her number.

"Yes, sure ..." she said. She fumbled through her shiny black leather bag for a pen and piece of paper.

"Well, thank you for the evening," I said as she handed me her number.

"Yes, I had a really good time," she said.

"Maybe we can go for a coffee next time?" I asked.

"I would like that."

"Well I'm going to take the bus home from here."

"Oh, alright. I'm going by subway."

Do I hug her now?
I'm pretty sure that's how it's done in Canada.
But this isn't Canada.

I bowed with a quick nod of my head as per the general cultural etiquette. She bowed back. She then blended into the throngs of sidewalk pedestrians hastily making their way to Shinchon subway station. I took a deep breath. I popped my dating cherry, finally, and my performance seemed to come off without a hitch.

6
Parentally Yours

OUR APARTMENT LANDLINE PHONE RANG just about every night, sometimes twice a day. My mom still agonized over our well-being, more than one year since Nunes and I first set foot in Seoul. She was especially concerned about our diets because we had moved out of our meals-included homestay rooms and now rented a compact two-bedroom apartment in Dangsan-Dong, a lower-middle class neighborhood.

One night, I heard Nunes on the phone in her room, which was adjacent to mine, mumbling something in Korean to Mom.

"Yonsei University is *mumble mumble mumble …*"

The words on which Nunes put emphatic stress managed to slither through the slight opening of her door, past the kitchen-*cum*-dining room and through the thin opening of my sliding glass door. The rest was muffled.

Silence.

"Yeah, I have a close friend who *mumble mumble mumble …*"

Silence.

"Seoul is too busy. I think *mumble mumble mumble …*"

Silence.

"Omma, how do you make fried rice?"

Of all the dishes Nunes made, my personal favorite was her spaghetti. The local grocery stores carried spaghetti noodles but not spaghetti sauce. Koreans used the noodles for other dishes, like *jja-jang myun* (noodles in black bean sauce). So Nunes copied what Weh-sook-mo, our aunt, would do – use ketchup instead. Heated, of course. The ketchup was a revelation; it injected the spaghetti with a tinge of tang. Nunes would add to the ketchup handfuls of the frozen mixed vegetables that we bought, like corn, green peas and carrots.

"Glen!" Nunes hollered. "Omma wants to talk to you."

I sat up on my colorful pin-striped *yo*, a traditional Korean futon. My eyes were dry, and I blinked a few times. I put down my introduction to anthropology textbook, along with my yellow highlighter, to the side of the *yo*, right next to my trusty dog-eared *Minjung* Korean-English dictionary. The back of my fingers brushed against the *ondol* floor as I lay down my textbook. I felt a warm sensation streak through the rest of my body. I then hauled myself up with both arms planted against the *yo* and headed next door.

"Hi, my dear son," my mom said in Korean. "Living in Seoul must be so hard, with so many people, no?"

"No, Omma, don't worry," I said, sliding back into the hard blue-and-white flower-printed couch that Weh-sook-mo had donated to us. Nunes lay on her *yo* with her back turned to me, her blanket pulled up to the top of her neck. It was only a little past 9 p.m. She was such an early bird.

"It's not *that* difficult. You get used to it," I said.

I did have one gripe, though. Two, actually.

"Whenever Nunes and I go to the market and haggle, or say something, Koreans always ask us where we're from. Or what region of Korea our accent came from."

My mom began laughing uncontrollably.

"When we say we're from Canada, they say, 'Oh ... you're a *kyopo*.'" A *kyopo* is an ethnic Korean who lives overseas, although it literally means a cell that lives in a stranger's body.

"And I do keep getting a lot of stink eye from Koreans on the buses and subway," I continued. "I think that's because I wear shorts outside when it gets hot. Not a lot of guys here do. Or maybe it's because I speak English with Nunes sometimes."

"Oh, be careful, my son. In Korea, speaking loudly in English in public places might be seen as conceited behavior. Like you're trying to show you're better than others. Are you eating right and helping out your Nuna?"

"Yeah, Nunes does all of the cooking, and it's surprisingly good," I said in an attempt at humor.

"And," I added, beaming with pride, "I do the dishes."

"You know that I worry a lot less because your Nuna is there. Are your classmates treating you alright? They're not arrogant because they're SNU students?"

"No, no, not at all. They're kind and very helpful. But they speak so fast that it's still difficult to catch everything they're saying. Oh ..." I paused. "They do make everyone give mini speeches every time we go out. It's as if they relish putting people on the spot." I guess I had three gripes in total tonight.

"*Stuh, stuh, stuh*," my mom said to express sympathy. "That must be nerve-wracking for you, I can only imagine."

A deep sense of guilt was palpable in my mom's voice. She had once told me that she didn't realize what she had done until it was too late, until Nunes and I were already gone, thousands of miles away from her side. The real possibility that our psychological or physical health could veer southward while living far away from home, trying to adjust to life in a foreign country, hit her hard. She still thought of us as her babies, even though Nunes was 21 and I was 19. And if things did go awry, my mom would be the one to blame, so she thought, since she was the one who planted the seed of coming here.

She also felt some heat from her Korean friends in Toronto. Instead of being impressed that her kids decided to return to the motherland to study, many of them couldn't understand why she encouraged us to live in a still-developing country when Canada was paradise – Korean students were dying to come here to study, they would say.

There was nothing I could do about that. I only hoped that, somewhere underneath that thick layer of guilt, my mom found solace in our ongoing metamorphoses. Nunes and I now both spoke almost entirely in Korean to her and my father on the phone. My Korean was rough around the edges, worse than Nunes', but there was a certain nuance to our communication now, certain Korean adjectives, like *so-seu-la-chi-da* ("flabbergasted"), and idiomatic expressions, like *gi-ga-mak-hyuh-suh* ("I was so dumbfounded that …"), that I used to drive home my emotional point better than before. And my mom would react in a screaming lyrical burst of laughter, surprised at how expressive I could be in her native tongue. I realized I had refrained from using more emotionally complex and informal words and idiomatic phrases when I spoke to her in English, lest she not understand. So I was beginning to shed my old Canadian skin and unfurl new, albeit very wet, Korean wings. I was Shakwon-izing before my mom's very ears.

My father would sometimes get on the line afterward. Our talks followed a familiar script:

> *Are you studying hard?*
>> Yes, I'm studying hard.
> *Remember that hard work, in the end, beats talent. How do you follow the lectures when they're in Korean?*
>> We use many English-language textbooks in class, my Korean-English dictionary never leaves my side and my classmates lend me their notes.
> *What are your marks like? Still the same?*
>> They are improving. My average is C+.
> *Well, just keep studying hard. Don't worry about money. Use my Visa card whenever you need anything.*
>> Yes, I will.

There were times my father would veer off script – usually when he had a few drinks in him – and, in a bout of nostalgia, reveal more tidbits about his past.

"You know," he once said, "when I was your age, I was already serving in the military."

"Oh, really?" He probably told me a long time ago, but I had forgotten.

"Oh, yeah," he said, his voice rising. "Back then, we had to serve three years. I spent some of that time patrolling the North-South Demilitarized Zone. There, in the dead of night, North Korean spies would come up from behind and slit the throats of South Korean soldiers. I never knew when I could be next."

"Oh, wow, I did not know that."

"Yes, it's true. Anyway ... put your Nuna on the phone."

7

A Mantra is Born

"No," SHE SAID.

"Really?" I said.

"Well, highly unlikely."

These three words stung. And, no, this wasn't a scene from one of my dates (although it could very well have been). The words came out of the mouth of the English department secretary. I was starting my last semester of my second year at SNU, and I asked her whether I could now apply to switch majors.

Ms. Yang was always a warm and stabilizing voice, my anchor, amidst the hostile world of a new and different school culture. She would patiently respond to the tens of questions I had about the complex world of student policies and registration procedures, and she'd reassure me everything was going to be okay. On this chilly November morning in 1993, however, her words sounded like cancer to my ears.

According to university policy, as Ms. Yang carefully explained to me, I could only switch majors if there was an opening – in other words, a student had dropped out – in the department to which I wanted to transfer, which was about as rare as an albino lion. The only other option was to re-apply for admission into the preferred program and start over again in Year 1, and that's *if* I got accepted a second time after another interview examination.

I walked out of our administrative office into the dim and empty basement hallway of the Humanities building. My face felt droopy. I hauled my body up a flight of stairs, plodding one step after another. Once outside, I was blinded by the last rays of the setting sun, but I didn't flinch. I wasn't in a hurry, and I wasn't going in any particular direction.

I made my way down the winding landscaped paths. I walked past a collection of concrete structures that dwarfed passersby. Hidden just beyond the walls' concrete

47

thickness were, I imagined, department offices and classrooms teeming with life, clusters of freshmen, sophomores, juniors and seniors engaged in exuberant chatter or listening wide-eyed to the lecturing professor, oblivious to the miracle of fluid communication and fat in the knowledge bright futures awaited them all.

I kept walking. The campus was sprawled out over a vast plot of sloping land that stretched more than 1,000 acres, along the southern edges of the city. It was a wonderful place to get lost and clear your head. After a good 30 minutes, I meandered my way down to the foot of the hills and to the university entrance. I boarded the 303 bus there and took a seat at the back. I was lucky that SNU was the first stop (or last, depending on your vantage point) on the 303 route because I was guaranteed a seat for the 25-minute ride home.

Once the bus rumbled back into the streets of Seoul and its 10 million residents, it filled up with sardined riders in short order. I looked out the window. Honking Hyundai hatchbacks and Kia sedans everywhere, darting across four lanes and through the tightest of spaces as though driving was a video game. Streaks of red and yellow-pink neon lights illuminating the crosses atop church buildings and signage of tiny storefronts, respectively. High-rise apartment buildings rubbing elbows, hilly back-alley roads, the odd skyscraper. The violating smell of bus exhaust. Sudden stops and starts. My head started pounding. At least no one has burped up kimchi yet, I thought to myself, exasperated. This had happened to me before. The sulfuric stench of salted shrimps, cabbage and garlic marinated in stomach gas lingered longer with so many people and so little ventilation.

I returned my gaze to the people on the bus. Lots of bodily contact and some pushing aside. Besides the odd scowl, most passengers didn't bat an eyelid when they were shoved. I understood them. With so many people crammed together in one city, "excuse me" or "sorry" was indeed a waste of breath and energy because it would happen again tomorrow. And the day after that. And the day after that day.

Did something get lost in translation? I thought to myself as I sat there on the raised leather bench seat at the back of the bus, with my knapsack on my lap and both hands placed on top of it. I was certain that the SNU admissions guy told me I'd have no problem changing programs after my second year. Was there some miscommunication between us, due to the language barrier? I should have made doubly sure. I shouldn't have assumed SNU would be like any university in Canada, where you didn't have to decide on a major until year two.

I was able to tough it out my first two years in the English department by often reminding myself that my dream of studying Oriental philosophy was just around the corner. I would soon be rewarded. This, in turn, would rekindle heartening visions of the wise Oriental philosopher who would go on to enlighten the world. All of a sudden, in the span of a few minutes, years of dreaming and wonderfully imagined scenarios crashed and burst into flames. Not unlike my hockey career.

I didn't want to start over again in Year 1, no matter how many transfer credits I could get. I would still lose all of the credits for the English major courses I took, and they comprised the bulk of them. I worked too hard just to pass those courses to simply let them go like that. It would also mean I'd be away from home even longer than I expected.

My mind raced in search of other options. *Should I leave Seoul National and apply to another university in the city?*

No, of course not. That would be the same as starting over in Year 1 at SNU. Moreover, I'd again have to suffer through the emotional roller-coaster of being the new foreign kid on campus.

Should I just quit altogether and go back to Toronto?

No. I vowed to my family and friends back home that I would accomplish the feat of completing a Bachelor's degree in a foreign country and language, and I didn't want to lose face when I returned home. Then again, if I told them I finished my degree in English from Korea, there wouldn't be much face to save. That would be equivalent to a native Korean student going abroad to study Korean at a Canadian university. It could be perceived as a cop-out.

I told my mom the bad news over the phone that night. My mom's voice dropped to a whisper.

"Really? ... There're no other possibilities?"

"No ... I don't think so."

"Maybe," she said, "someone might drop out between now and the beginning of the new semester next year ... You never know, no?"

"I doubt it. There's not much time left ..."

My mom's tone of voice soon shot right back up.

"As Master Daehaeng says, always believe in the True Self, the Foundation within you," she said. "Trust this Foundation. It knows better than you."

"Okay," I said, unsure exactly what she meant. I guessed that she meant I should always believe in myself and my deeper latent potential.

My mom was eager to dispense to Nunes and me the teachings of Master Daehaeng, a Korean Buddhist nun who was the founder and spiritual leader of the Hanmaum Zen Center in Korea, after The Epiphany.

The Epiphany was the stuff of lore in my family. The stuff of lore in a roll-ing-your-eyes kind of way, that is. We had heard it so often. Three years ago my mom's cousin and fellow Buddhist lent her a book by Master Daehaeng. My mom devoured the book in a day, slapped her hands together and said, "This is it!" Mas-ter Daehaeng's teachings spoke to her like no Korean Buddhist teacher before her. She then put the book down and, on the spot, faced the direction of Korea and prostrated three times, tears streaming down her cheeks. Master Daehaeng's words had solved the riddle of suffering for her, the suffering that came from moving away from family, friends and home in her 30s just so she could live in a stranger's land, speak a strange language and not have time to raise and educate her children the way she imagined she would. The strain that these conditions put on married life brought her to a boiling point.

"All things happen for a reason. A greater reason," she continued. "So hardships are actually there to make you grow."

This struck a chord with me. I did find the opposing notion that painful experiences have no deeper underlying meaning, or nothing to teach me, too unilateral and rigid in thinking – not to mention depressing – for my tastes. I knew that, at the very least, I grew stronger from my experiences at SNU. I developed more inner fortitude. What doesn't kill you makes you stronger, no? I remembered one particular line from Shunryu Suzuki's *Zen Mind, Beginner's Mind*, a book I had bought at Kyobo Bookstore one month after I first arrived in Seoul. Suzuki called the distractions and difficulties people experience in sitting meditation Mind Weeds. Just as we "pull the weeds and bury them near the plant to give it nourishment," you should "rather be grateful for the weeds you have in your mind, because they will eventually enrich your practice."

After we hung up, I experimented with making my own personal mantra.

> *These difficult experiences living in Korea have helped me to grow, to build my character.*
> *Maybe these "gains" will come in handy in the future, even though I might not see it now.*

That was the aspirin I needed. I immediately felt better. Gratitude replaced hopelessness, and I continued with this line of thinking.

I thought about the English department. I wondered whether I'd be where I was today, having passed all my courses to date, if not for my department. The list of readings for my major courses included the likes of the Norton Anthology of English Literature, the Transcendentalist writings of Emerson and Thoreau, a number of Shakespeare's plays and a slew of other English-language classics. I was often allowed to write my essay assignments in English. Had I studied philosophy with a focus on Eastern, I could only imagine how many more Korean-language books and essays I would have had to read and write, and how many courses I'd have failed in the process. *Could this be one of those "greater reasons"?* And I did fall in love with Thoreau's *Walden*. Thoreau didn't play by the rules. He left civilization behind to live alone in the woods with only the bare essentials, in service to a greater destiny, to a transformed perspective and thinking that wasn't enslaved to ancient prejudices or the "common mode of living." Walden, at times, felt like the only true friend I had in Seoul, and he'd speak to me in between the lines. He reassured me that my time in Korea, my adventures in the wilderness of a new culture, was far from wasted; it was a noble act of disobedience.

My classmates were a special group. They would share with me the intel they had gathered from our *sunbaes* about certain courses and professors and their testing tendencies, whether for our major courses or electives.

"Glen, quick, come here," my classmates would say to me with concurrent waves of their hands in the days leading up to exam week. I would usually bump into huddles of them in the student lounge area inside our department office or just outside the building by the benches.

"Make a note of this," one of them would say, as if someone among them had found the lost map that led to untold amounts of treasure.

I didn't ask why or how. They were much more in the know than I was. I simply focused on the chapters and pages of the textbooks they suggested. The intel must have been good because I always passed. My marks weren't stellar, normally in the mid 'C' range, but I didn't care. My mind was in full survival mode – both academically and emotionally – and the academic standards I held myself to in high school were but a mirage at this point.

Would I have met an equally caring set of classmates had I gone to the philosophy department?
Would I have lasted this long at SNU if not for the English department?
Believe, Glen.

8
Wanted: Enlightenment

I TURNED INTO THE DRIVEWAY OF THE Hanmaum Zen Center of Toronto on Glencairn in my father's old blue boat, the Pontiac Parisienne. I reached for the transmission stick at the steering wheel, switched to "P" and turned off the ignition.

The 15-minute drive over from my parents' place was easier than I thought: I had inched along through the naked roads and cruised along the main streets under the cover of the night sky, mindful of the snowy and slippery conditions and my blind spots, as my father instructed before handing over the keys. Even though I got my license back in high school, I was still a rookie since I never drove in Seoul.

I had driven the Pontiac on my own a few times before, whenever I visited Toronto during the winter break, but driving it this December felt different. It felt like my own car, like my father was about to gift it to me, for successfully completing my English degree at SNU a few weeks ago. I guess I was hoping this would be my graduation gift.

I felt the sting of the minus-13 degrees Celsius weather on my face after I stepped out of the car. I zipped up my long navy blue coat and turned my collar up as I walked up the steps to the front door of an old bungalow stucco house. That's how most Korean Buddhist temples or centers in Toronto started out. They rented or bought spaces in office buildings or purchased small homes in lower middle-class residential neighborhoods because they lacked the membership – and hence deep pockets – to purchase a larger building. Hanmaum was the most recent addition to the small Korean Buddhist scene in the city. Yes, it fell under the spiritual leadership of Master Daehaeng and, of course, it was the center that my parents regularly attended.

The door to the center was unlocked, and I let myself in. I took my shoes off and sat down on the carpeted floor of the Main Dharma Hall, which was probably once someone's living room.

I had made an appointment to meet with Chongwol Sunim, whom I briefly met earlier in the day after the morning Sunday service. My mom had told me about him upon my return to Toronto, that one of the two monks living at the center was like me – a young Korean who grew up in the West (the U.S., in his case), was around my age (a few years older, to be more precise) and journeyed to Korea, only in his case to enter the monkhood. He had apparently also studied at Maharishi University in Iowa – a school founded by Maharishi Mahesh Yogi – and once spent months meditating in a cave in the Himalayas, subsisting on small rations of goat milk, living with scorpions as his roommates and Indian yogis as his neighbors. And I thought what I did was unique. Oh, did I mention he was also fluent in English and Korean? I felt I had finally met a kindred spirit. I knew he was someone I had to talk to about my interest in studying Oriental philosophy.

A few minutes later Chongwol Sunim emerged from his living quarters adjacent to the Main Dharma Hall. He clasped his hands and bowed slightly toward the enshrined gilt Buddha statue to his right. Once he turned to face me, I was a deer in headlights, caught staring into the eyes of a stone-faced lion staring down his prey. His eyelids looked swollen, like a battered retired boxer. I could see fumes emanating from the top of his head, which was the size of a basketball (and with it shaved, it looked like one). His ear lobes were long and thick, his shoulders broad and rounded and his stomach large and protruding.

As he swaggered toward me in his light grey monastic jacket and baggy cotton pants, I couldn't help but think he looked eerily like the "Laughing Buddha" statue that sat on the cashier counters at Chinese restaurants in Toronto. He was a lion dressed in monk's clothing.

"Come with me," he said, looking straight ahead. "I'll brew us some tea."

I followed him down the stairs and to the basement kitchen. I grabbed the traditional Korean tea set that was on top of a food tray and he an electric tea kettle and massive metal kettle of water, and we both went back upstairs.

We sat down in the middle of the room. Sunim poured some water into the electric kettle and plugged it into the nearest socket. He then shoveled a handful of fresh crispy green tea leaves from a small silver bag into the teapot. I sat there facing him with my hands on my lap, waiting patiently. I looked up at the ceiling, down at my lap, side to side and at him. I could hear the whirring of the kettle as it warmed up.

Sunim didn't look at me once. He sat in silence. His mouth was closed and his gaze lowered. He breathed heavily through his nostrils, the rhythm of which was violently broken a couple of times when he would clear his throat with a thunderous roar.

The kettle started to gurgle. Before long, it reached a crescendo and then – "click." He reached for the kettle and, holding up the wide drooping sleeves of his jacket with his other hand, he proceeded to gently pour the steaming water into the ceramic cooling bowl without spilling or splashing a drop. After letting it sit for a couple of minutes, he poured the contents of the bowl into the teapot to infuse the tea leaves inside in the hot water. Precise water temperature and timing was everything if you wanted to avoid bitter or bland-tasting tea and, within moments, he poured the tea into two off-white palm-sized ceramic cups that had been patiently waiting off to the side.

"That's *really* good," I said after taking a sip. It had a smooth nutty flavor. I began to understand why it was called a tea ceremony rather than simply "tea time." I wrapped the cup in both my hands, and its warmth felt like a pair of woolen reading socks on a winter's night.

"Yeah, it's not bad," he said, smiling. He then readied the next cup by pouring more of the boiled water into the cooling bowl.

I told him about my English degree at SNU. "But, as my mom probably told you, I'm interested in studying Oriental philosophy, like Buddhism," I said. "I don't know a lot about it, though. I mean, my mom tells me about Master Daehaeng's teachings although I don't always understand …"

"That's okay," he said immediately. "When you don't understand a Buddhist teaching, store the teaching in a 'bag.' When your level of understanding later matches that level of teaching, you'll understand it."

What a pragmatic answer. I was impressed he didn't tee off on a dogmatic tangent and lecture me on Buddhism 101. I sensed that he was drawing from his "been there, done that" personal experience, which was the kind of honesty I preferred and had hoped to hear. His advice was simply "don't get attached to even not knowing."

We both took another sip of our tea.

"If you want to study Buddhism the right way," he said, "you should go back to Korea to do your Master's."

"Really? But I want to stay in Canada."

"Why?"

"Because, well, I miss my family and friends and …"

Sunim crinkled his nose as if he had just bitten into a lemon.

"Oh, boy, you're still just a kid," he said with a discernible tinge of contempt in his voice.

He reminded me of my father in that moment. I didn't respond. The puffed pride I carried with me, knowing what I had endured for four long years in Korea, had just been punched in the gut.

"Well, if *that's* the reason you don't wanna go back," he said somewhat sarcastically, "there's nothing I can do about that …"

He was right. If I didn't want to return to Korea simply because I missed the comforts of home, that was a cowardly reason and certainly not the mark of a great man. And I wanted to fulfill my destiny and be great.

I was curious about one thing, though.

"Where would I study in Korea? Besides, I think you need a B.A. in religion or philosophy to do a Master's at Seoul National."

"I don't think Dongguk requires that, but you might have to do some make-up courses."

Huh? Dongguk?

I had heard about the university long ago but dismissed it out of hand as some small obscure college in Seoul. When Sunim proceeded to describe it, however, I turned those preconceptions on their head; I began to envision a mystical Shangri-La, a place teeming with wise and enlightened Buddhist ascetics who sprayed the campus air with the scent of mysticism and wisdom.

Coincidentally, Sunim would be moving on to live in a mountain monastery in Korea soon. He invited me to stay and study Buddhism there for a few months to prep for grad school, if I decided to go to Dongguk.

I tossed and turned when I went to bed that evening. I wanted to be like Sunim and learn from him, through osmosis if I had to. I wanted to be sure of myself and ooze confidence – not to mention machismo – like him. I once had a dream, but grey clouds presently hovered over it, now that I had an English degree. I was still a boy in search of an identity, and the pricking at the back of my head by this uncertainty never let up.

I then wondered how much of Sunim's aura of assuredness stemmed from his lifestyle as a Buddhist monk. I knew about the sacrifices monks made – no more of those giddy feelings of being in love, no kids of your own, no possibility of fame. Imagine the benefits of these sacrifices, though, I thought. By simply letting go of all these things, there'd be no more stress. No longer would I need to go on a wild goose chase in search of a career and identity. Wouldn't confidence, a deep abiding contented kind of confidence, naturally flow from not wanting? I'd live a very simple and self-sufficient way of life – *Walden*. Then there was the promise of some kind of spiritual enlightenment in the end, which would put me in a perpetual state of bliss. If I meditated under the one-on-one tutelage of Sunim, deep in the mountains, I could achieve it. I could feel it in the marrow of my bones.

The prospects of returning to Seoul and more inconveniences and stressors did cross my mind a few times. My Korean had improved drastically, but was it at a graduate level? Could I stand to be away from family and friends for another two years, minimum? I would be alone this time: Nunes had completed her Bachelor's degree in biology at the same time as me, and there was no doubt she was going to stay in Toronto for good. I would no longer have anyone to shoot the shit with, in English, when I came home. But my heart wanted what it wanted, and it wanted to live in Shangri-La and enlightenment.

I started to piece together my life story and its epic ending in my head:

> Jaded by the emotional emptiness of a secular career, I return to one of the Asian heartlands of Buddhism and to the mystical training grounds of Korean Buddhist monks.
>
> I immerse myself in their environment and absorb their abilities to quiet and free the mind from the chains of emotional attachment.
>
> Yearning to go deeper into my meditative practice, however, I descend into the utter solitude and quietude of the mountains.
>
> Just me and one set of the traditional light-grey Buddhist robe and winter hat.

I live off the grid in a hermitage and off the wild fruits of the land and raw vegetables that I grow on a small adjacent plot of land. I feel at one with nature and a deep sense of satisfaction from being self-sufficient.

As rumor spreads among local villagers about the curious young man living in meditative solitude in the mountains, people from as far away as the cities make the trek up the steep treacherous path to see me in the hopes they might take away a nugget of spiritual wisdom with them.

I felt that familiar warm and fuzzy emotion of discovery, of having found my destiny and calling in life once again. I decided then and there that I would return to Korea. Even if I could accomplish only a fragment of my dreams, I'd be well on my way to true happiness.

I waited for my parents to return home from work before telling them about my decision to study at Dongguk (the Buddhist monkhood idea would have to wait until after I gave the Master's a shot.) My parents now managed a post office after graduating from the corner store business a year ago, although they still owned the property and would continue to live above the store.

"Oh, really?" my mom said with slumped shoulders, her face a pale hue. It was 5:30 p.m., and she had just come in the door.

She put her bag down on the pasty blue half-moon sectional couch, which – no matter how many times I thought about it – never served its intended purpose of complementing our sprawling chestnut sofa adjacent to it.

My mom's response was tempered. She's probably just tired, I thought.

"Well, yes," she said, sliding off her long and bulky brown wool coat, "studying

Oriental philosophy was something you originally wanted to do."

She rolled up her sleeves, ready to head to the kitchen. But she took both my hands in hers.

"But are you *sure* you can handle living away from home, for two more years?" she said, staring deep into my eyes, as though they might give away my secrets, namely that I was really doing this to please her.

"Yes, Omma," I said, rolling my eyes. My mom had this ability to make my eyes roll like no one else.

I could tell she was torn. On the one hand, she didn't want to see her baby suffer more hardships living alone and in a foreign country.

On the other hand, I was certain the wan face masked the joy. Not only would I be continuing my cultural journey in the motherland, I'd be pursuing the study of Buddhism, the teachings of which brought out my mom's pious side. She believed Buddhism offered answers to the one and only thing that mattered in life – true inner peace. And it was this inner peace that led to the ultimate Buddhist goal of liberation from the cycle of birth and death and, hence, more suffering.

It was as though my mom had begun to see the world anew. Everything that happened to us in our lives was but a karmic hurdle that we were meant to leap over. Time was also of the essence. It was only through a human life that liberation was possible, and one lifetime goes by in the blink of an eye, my mom would warn me. So Buddhist practice was way more important for her children than finding a cushy job, raising a happy family and owning a house with a white-picket fence. She wasn't your typical Korean mother in that sense. In fact, my mom mentioned in passing once that she "wouldn't mind" if I ever decided to join the brotherhood of monks one day.

My father was simply happy that I wanted to move on to do a higher degree, even if it was at Dongguk, which was considered a class below SNU in academic rank.

"It's good to specialize," he said that evening as he entered my room. I was lying down on my bed, watching a Leafs game on the rice cooker-sized miniature TV that sat atop my drawer chest. I lowered the volume because his narrowed eyes were laser-like, and I sensed he wanted this to be a serious father-son moment.

"You know," he went on, "the key to success is to be the best in *one thing*. You will never starve if you do. Read a lot of books and study hard, as though you live in the library. I will support you 100 percent. Don't worry about money." Deep down I knew I was both blessed and spoiled. I rationalized the guilt of the latter by vowing to myself that I would repay him one day, by going on to do great things.

Heejeh was home one night – a rarity. She'd gone out most evenings since her return home for the March study break from McGill University in Montreal, where she was a freshman studying – of all things – English literature (I had nothing to do with it).

I knocked on the plastic sliding doors of her room. A few seconds later – *rrriiippp*!

"Oh, hey …" she said in a perky voice. She turned around to go back to her desk, leaving the door open.

I sat down at the edge of her bed.

"So I'm going back to Korea in a couple of weeks, eh?"

"Yeah, I *knoooow* ..." she said as she turned to face me, the long strands of her black hair sliding over to shade her slender jawline. Her black eyes sparkled with disbelief.

"You're *crazy* to go back. I can't imagine doing that." Her right hand remained stationary atop the desk, gripping a pen; she had been doodling something on a pad of paper.

I hadn't seen much of my little sis in the past four years. University life seemed to have mellowed her out. The Heejeh I knew was more bubbly, not to mention restless. She also looked more and more like Nunes, albeit a 3-inch shorter version of her.

"Well," I said, raising my eyebrows, "if you want to study Buddhism, that's the sacrifice you have to make."

"And that's just you, I guess," she said. "When you do something, you get all obsessed about it."

Her last words hung in the air.

"That's true, I guess, eh?" I never thought of it that way, that, instead of passionate, which was the position I took, my behavior could be interpreted as obsessive.

9
Monastic Myths

IT WAS 3:30 A.M. WHEN I WAS AWOKEN FROM my slumber. I heard the faint sounds of a Buddhist monk chanting as he slowly meandered his way around the monastery grounds and past the rooms of its sleepy residents.

Striking a *moktak* (a bubble-shaped wooden percussion instrument not much bigger than the size of one's hand) with a small wooden mallet, the monk's voice sliced the silence of this secluded monastery, tucked in the foothills of Mt. Oryong in Korea, 90 minutes and a world apart from the bright lights of Seoul. The voice was beckoning residents to come join him in the early morning service.

The chanting and beating grew louder. The monk was approaching my room, and the moment he did I opened my eyes to catch a glimpse of his silhouette as it glided past the wooden lattice-framed glass doors. I got out of bed bleary-eyed, crawled to the door and put my nose to the glass. I saw the figure of the monk fade into the pre-dawn darkness, and along with him dissipated the sounds of his voice and the echoed beat of the *moktak*.

There was something very moving about this experience. The monk was the unsung hero in the story of Korean Buddhism, a solitary figure wading through the darkness, expressing his faith and performing his duties when no one was looking.

Still, it was 3 damn 30 in the morning!

I crawled back to the toasty warmth of my *yo*, which had overnight absorbed the radiant floor heating. I pulled my blanket over my shoulders as I stayed sitting for several minutes.

I rubbed my eyes.

"Shit, even prepared, this is going to be a lot harder than I thought," I said, yawning.

Still half awake, I put on my winter jacket to head over to the Main Dharma Hall, which was a short cascade of blocks of stones away from my room. There was no time to brush my teeth or wash up – the nearest washroom was in the office building across the courtyard.

I was jolted out of my sleepy stupor as soon as I stepped outside. The crisp, pine tree-laced mountain air hit me like a whiff of smelling salts. How refreshing, I thought. I shuddered to think of all the fumes that emanated from the hundreds of smoke stacks and the more than two million car exhausts in Seoul, which I had ingested over the past four years.

I slipped off my shoes at the side entrance to the Hall. I was welcomed by mostly empty rows of rectangular brown mats strewn across the polished wooden flooring. I picked my spot in the last row on the right side of the Hall, where the men were supposed to sit. Women sat on the left side. I prostrated three times on my mat in the direction of the altar, as per the temple etiquette, and sat down. The layer of frost that had formed overnight on the mat seeped through my jeans and stung my flesh. My body convulsed in response.

I put my hands in my jacket pocket and hunched my shoulders. I could see my breath and hear the beat of my heart. I scanned the room. A scattering of laity, all with eyes closed and heads bowed, kneeled or sat cross-legged on their mats. They were probably out-of-towners who stayed the night. A row of monks kneeled at the front. They draped chestnut brown cloaks over their usual and more casual light grey robes. Directly in front of them hovered the altar, on top of which calmly sat a looming gilt statue of the Buddha, who glinted under the ceiling lights and illuminated amidst the intricately embossed wood carvings of past Korean Zen masters in the backdrop. The Buddha's expression never seemed to change. As always, calm and smiling, even at this ungodly hour, I thought with a smirk.

One of the monks slowly picked himself up and walked off to the side, where sat a large black bronze bell hung on a wooden beam. He knelt before it and waited for a moment. The monk then grabbed the thick mallet that lay there and began striking the bell in soft rapid succession, building up to a crescendo and thunderous reverberating sounds. The service was well on its way.

"Ma ha banya bara milda shimgyung ..."

We were now chanting the *Heart Sutra*, a much-beloved scripture in Korean Buddhism (and the Buddhisms of East Asia in general). I welcomed the song: I knew from my time at the center in Toronto that it marked the end of the service, which meant I could go back to my room to sleep soon.

When the service ended, we prostrated three more times and meditated for several minutes (some longer). I then picked myself and my aching knees up off the mat and immediately returned to my room to squeeze in about an hour of extra sleep before I had to get up again, clean up and be at the communal kitchen for breakfast by 6 a.m. sharp. (If you missed breakfast, there would be nothing to eat until lunchtime.)

The communal dining hall, a large space fitted with a series of long, dark brown rectangular eating tables, was divided into two sections at mealtimes – one half for

Buddhist monastics and the other half for the laity. Sunim and I ate at separate tables. The monastery only served vegetarian fare, usually a combination of sticky white rice, different vegetarian soups and side dishes of seasoned vegetables. Kimchi was a staple side dish, of course.

Once I finished eating, Sunim came over to my table, put his hand on my shoulder and said to meet him on the second floor of the office building. I returned my food tray to the kitchen counter and went straight upstairs. The second floor opened up into a cavernous and carpeted hall. I saw a piano in the near right corner and a large sagging plastic bag at the front. Along the left wall sat one wooden folding table with two chairs placed on either side. The place was as empty and hollow as it was wide and spacious. It's probably used for lay activities on special days, I thought. I took off my shoes, walked over to the table and sat down.

A few minutes later, *thump, thump*. Sunim had arrived. He came armed with a few books in his hand.

"Have a look," he said as he sat down and slid the books he was holding to my side of the table.

"Your goal is to finish this exercise book on learning *hanmun* and memorize 1,000 characters while you're here."

He gave me a lot to digest in a span of five seconds. *Hanmun* meant classical Chinese, I knew. But how many did he say?

"Oh, 1,000? Wow, that's a lot," I said.

"Well, that's the minimum you'll need to know for Dongguk," he said, his enlarged pupils daring me to defy him. "If you start Dongguk in September, that doesn't leave us much time."

Buddhist studies at Dongguk, Sunim explained, favored the study of the Buddhist sutras (scriptures) written in the original classical Chinese. If that was the case, I did, indeed, have a lot of catching up to do. I knew that native Koreans could read and write close to 2,000 classical Chinese characters by the time they graduated high school. They had to – approximately 60 percent of Korean words originate from the Chinese. I couldn't imagine how many more thousands my future graduate school colleagues knew by now. I, on the other hand, knew zero.

"We're going to study *hanmun* together," Sunim said. He was sorting out the books on the table, heavily breathing through his nose.

"Oh, okay …" I said. I tried to contain my surprise.

He looked up at me: "As a Buddhist monk, I have to know *hanmun*, too. I'm a beginner just like you." For the first time, I saw Sunim in a vulnerable light.

We spent the rest of the day in our chairs reading, writing and reciting aloud one character at a time, each at our own pace, only leaving our seats to attend the Dharma services and *gongyang* (meals weren't called meals here; they were *gongyang* – offerings to the community of living cells existing in the body).

In fact, that was how I would spend the coming days and weeks:

Morning schedule
3:30 – Wake up
4 – Early morning Dharma service
6 – Breakfast *gongyang*
7 – Study Chinese characters
10 – Morning Dharma service

Afternoon schedule
12 noon – Lunch *gongyang*
1 – Study Chinese characters
5 – Afternoon Dharma service

Evening schedule
6 – Dinner *gongyang*
7 – Study Chinese characters
9-10 – Lights out

I held onto the hope that Chongwol Sunim would one day hurl fireballs of wisdom from his breath that would crack open the egg that held me hostage. Or assign me passages to read from scriptures that would make my eyes expand and pupils dilate. Or set me up on a rigorous sitting meditation regimen that punished the body but tamed the mind. I would then come to focus and live in the present moment like Sunim, overflow with confidence and be contented like him. That would be my enlightenment, my moment of personal liberation and freedom.

But that day never came. Instead, Sunim sat next to me with pen in hand and head buried in our exercise book. Instead, I stared at straight and squiggly lines all day, like this one: 洪. And this one: 荒. I felt like Ralph Macchio in *The Karate Kid*, and Sunim was Mr. Miyagi. Instead of "wax on, wax off," I was muttering "Sky is *Chun* (天), earth is *Ji* (地)", and on it went. And Mr. Miyagi, in this case, was learning to wax on and off alongside me.

By the fourth week, I started spending long stretches of the day alone in the hall. Sunim was called to do other projects for the monastery, including the publication of a comprehensive Korean-English dictionary of Buddhist terms. He would pop in throughout the day to check up on me.

On special days, I got to assist him on his other work, which broke up the daily monotony. On *very* special days, Sunim would thump into the room between 8 p.m. and 9 p.m., wearing only a white short-sleeve shirt on top of his sagging grey baggy pants, his lips stretched into the shape of a Half Moon that squished his cheeks into round balls, holding a plate of food in one hand. The senior monks had ordered (vegetarian) pizza from the local pizzeria as a late night snack, and he had a few slices for me.

I used my 30-minute post-*gongyang* breaks to stroll around the monastery grounds. The first time I did so, I realized I hadn't taken the time to catch my breath, stand back and soak in Gwangmyung Zen Center's enormity and intricacies. It was but one of several domestic branches of the main Hanmaum Center, which was headquartered in Anyang near Seoul. Multiple traditional Korean buildings were cloistered together on acres of mountain foothills, engulfed by clusters of towering green pine trees. Perched atop the monastery was the Main Dharma Hall, covered in earthy-brown paint, roofed by upward-curving tile eaves that were undergirded by an intricate pattern of shamrock green, blood red and bright orange, and bridged to the rest of the monastery grounds by granite steps, at the bottom of which sat two small statues of guardian lions on either side. The lions each "screened" you before you were allowed to enter. When I passed them, I imagined they screened for self-esteem, hence their menacing countenance.

Off to the left of the Main Dharma Hall loomed a 6-meter-tall block of white granite carved in the form of the Buddha of Compassion, welcoming visitors to the monastery with her right hand raised and palm facing forward. A few stone steps up from the statue sat an elongated single-story traditional Korean structure, at the center of which was the private living quarters of the abbot of the temple. On either side of his room were two smaller rooms, one of which I was fortunate enough to stay in.

I turned and walked down a slope for about 50 meters, toward the entrance. There, off to the right, on a plot of land about three acres in size, lay row upon row of hundreds of granite pagodas that memorialized three immediately preceding generations of ancestors of monastery adherents. It was the Buddhist version of a cemetery.

I turned again and walked back up the slope to the main office building. In the recesses of this red brick building were the private living quarters of more than 20 in-training novice and senior monks. They were religious elite who had forsaken family and worldly pleasures in order to devote themselves to a life of mental and spiritual discipline and discovery. Laity were not allowed in.

On the first floor, by the communal kitchen, was a large room where the few full-time resident staff members, who helped with the cooking and other labor, such as building maintenance, slept. On most days, the number of monastics far outnumbered the number of visiting lay adherents from the nearest town.

Because of this the Gwangmyung Zen Center had an austere, regimented and military-like ambience about it: there were strict rules of conduct and etiquette, and there was a schedule of religious services (three per day) and *gongyang* times that visitors, guests and resident monks alike were required to follow. Chongwol Sunim was like my drill sergeant who ensured I kept to these rules and schedule.

I had always imagined the mountain temples as a rural spiritual resort of sorts, where visitors could come to escape the stress and chaos of the city. There, we would bask in the beauty of the green hovering over and around us, sit in meditative repose or engage in the finer pursuits of life, such as calligraphy or profound philosophical discussions about the meaning of life, while sipping on a steaming ceramic cup of green tea.

I was wrong.

The only monastics I saw out and about were the novice monks, discernible by their all-brown robes. They never seemed to be without some menial task or chore to do, be it cooking, cleaning, sweeping, lifting or fixing something. They worked side by side with the few full-time lay staff members. At least they were active, I thought, in constant motion and producing endorphins, instead of sitting on a chair and reading and writing all day – the longer I stayed at the monastery, the closer I grew to Chongwol Sunim in weight.

Rare were the occasions I bumped into one of the senior monks, who didn't often venture outside of their living quarters. I imagined they engaged in intense meditation sessions in their rooms or, like Sunim, worked on large projects for the monastery. When I did run into one of them, they were usually short on small talk:

"Hello, Sunim," I would say with a bow and palms clasped. That was the Korean way of greeting fellow Buddhists.

"Yes, hello," the senior monk would respond, palms together.

"So I hear you're staying with us for a while."

"Yes, I am."

"How are you enjoying it so far?"

"I'm learning a lot."

"Wonderful. Well, good luck, *Beobunim* (Dharma Brother)."

"Thank you."

The senior monk would return to his room and I upstairs to the second floor.

When Chongwol Sunim came upstairs to visit me one morning, I remarked on how surprised I was at the busyness of everybody here. "If you find you have time on your hands here," he said, "you have too much time."

I was given the weekends off. For the first month, I used that time to return to Seoul and check on the apartment I was renting. When Sunim instructed me to stay in town on weekends so as to minimize unnecessary distractions, I began to feel trapped and claustrophobic.

So one Saturday I decided to trek down to the nearest town, a good 20 minutes by foot, in search of civilization. When I arrived, empty stores and eateries lined the town's main stretch of street. The commercial buildings stood a few stories tall, exteriors discolored from the accumulated dust and dirt. Cars swished by every so often. On the sidewalks, I saw the odd person or couple dart in and out of the local mom-and-pop shops and restaurants. Not one Western fast food chain in sight. Not even McDonald's. Compared to the flashing neon signs, skyscrapers and hustle and bustle of Seoul, the town was forlorn and silent.

I put on a brave face and willed myself through the first two months at the monastery. When doubts about whether I was truly happy here crept into my head, I shoved them right back down from whence they came, with both arms. I reminded myself that I was living my dream and, hence, I *should* be thriving in this kind of an environment.

> *You're better than that, Glen.*
> *You're strong and independent.*
> *You've transcended trivial needs for companionship.*
> *Remember, you want to be like Sunim.*

I was living life at an elite level of denial. By the end of the second month, however, my true feelings could no longer be denied. They finally went rogue and demanded recognition: I was homesick.

Never mind Canada; I missed the comforts and amenities of Seoul – my own TV, seated toilets (I only had access to squatting toilets at the monastery), the bright lights and skyscrapers, the busy-bodies on the streets, the get-togethers and drinking nights with my SNU classmates, the mini speeches, the girls I dated and the seductive way they would run their fingers through their long silky black hair, some good old greasy American fast food …

I informed Sunim that I would stay the rest of the week but return to Seoul, for good, on the weekend.

10
Abstractions

PASSERS-BY ASSAULTED MY SHOULDERS AS I walked. Cars blared their horns behind me, ahead of me, to my left and to my right. Their exhaust filled the air and my nostrils. Neon lights blinded my eyes, and their remnant flashes danced along my cornea long after I arrived home.

Ah – it was good to be back in Seoul.

I was refreshed and looking forward to the courses at Dongguk. I had promptly applied to the Department of Seon (Zen) Studies when I returned from the monastery and received special admissions as a foreign student not too long after, with the proviso that I complete make-up courses, just as Sunim had predicted. I would begin my studies in a few months, in the fall of 1996.

I was eager to learn more about Zen after I recently bought and read *The Transmission of the Lamp* and *Zen Flesh, Zen Bones*, both classic Zen texts. I was grateful for the Kyobo Bookstore, which had a spacious and voluminous section of English-language books. The Chinese Ch'an (Chinese word for Zen) masters of yore featured in these stories shattered my image of Buddhist monks. They were wild, uninhibited and unpredictable, and I got to live vicariously through them.

I especially liked the story about the monk Pi Mo Yen, who seemed to think that becoming a monk was the work of the devil, although, if that was the case, it was, indeed, hypocritical considering the source.

> Venerable Pi Mo Yen of Wu T'ai Shan Monastery used to carry a wooden pitchfork with him. Every time he saw a monk approaching him and bowing down for instruction, he pinned him by the neck with the fork and demanded, "What devil forced you to renounce the world (by becoming a monk)? What devil made you wander on pilgrimage? If you can say a word of Ch'an under the fork, you will

die; if you can't say a word of Ch'an under the fork, you will die. Now! Say something!"

There were few students who were able to respond to this demand.

I didn't get the story's greater message, if there was one; I did, however, feel less guilty about not being able to hack the monastic lifestyle after reading this.

Dongguk's campus wasn't quite the mystical and fog-laced Shangri-La I had imagined. It was a typical modern Korean university campus that was dotted with drab grey and brown concrete buildings standing on hilly ground, much like SNU but half the territorial size. What differentiated Dongguk was a Main Dharma Hall building in the middle of the campus that stuck out like a red shirt because of its traditional Korean architecture, not to mention the occasional sighting of bald-headed students wearing the familiar grey monastic robes in the hallways. The vast majority of these monastics came from my department, where I was but one of three grad students who owned a full head of hair and a wardrobe that included non-grey items.

On the first day of classes, I discovered that the graduate curriculum was largely translation-based. For each course, a small group of us would take turns translating into Korean long passages from both classic and contemporary books on Buddhism, books mostly written in either classical Chinese or English. The training at the monastery came in handy after all.

For the rest of the hundreds of Chinese characters I was bound to come across but had not learned, I went to the university bookstore and bought an *Okpyun*, a Classical Chinese-Korean dictionary.

One by one, I picked up the basics of Buddhism as the weeks and months passed. I came to learn that many central Buddhist concepts were encased in numbers:

- 3 Jewels
- The 4 Noble Truths
- 4 Foundations of Mindfulness
- 5 Precepts
- The Noble 8-fold Path
- 8 Consciousnesses
- 12 Links of Dependent Origination

There was also a vast number of traditions and schools of thought in Buddhism – which threw my head for a loop because I thought they were essentially all one and the same:

- Mahayana (tradition existing mostly in East Asia)
- Theravada (tradition existing mostly in South Asia)
- Vajrayana (the main tradition in Tibet, Mongolia)
- Zen (a distinct school within Mahayana)
- Northern & Southern Schools of Ch'an
- Pure Land (a Mahayana school emphasizing rebirth in a Buddhist heaven)

And different styles of meditation:
- Zen Koans (meditation on cryptic sayings)
- Vipassana & Samatha (mindfulness)
- Tantra (visualizations involving union of energies)
- Zazen ("just sitting" meditation)
- Metta ("Loving-Kindness" meditation)

Different types of enlightenment, according to the Zen literature:
- Gradual enlightenment
- Sudden enlightenment

Concepts that seemed nihilistic and apocalyptic:
- Emptiness
- Nothingness
- True Self (and somehow No Self at the same time …)

And sayings cryptic in meaning and infuriating in solving:
- *Sees things as they really are*, one Theravada scholar-monk stated in characterizing the concentrated mind.
- *Mountains will again be mountains, rivers will again be rivers, the earth will be the earth, and the sky will be the sky*, a Zen Master wrote of the awakened mind.

My head was being stuffed with conceptual labels, categories and hierarchies. I was floating in a world of ideas, the spacy world of abstraction, anchor-less like an untethered astronaut slowly spinning away into the abyss. Instead of jumping out at me, the words on the page kept drifting like clouds, and I was constantly in a battle to pin them down, as though with Master Pi Mo Yen's wooden pitchfork. What ever happened to those stories about the iconoclastic Zen masters of yore, anyway? Those felt more real to me. Were we not going to read about them at some point? And didn't these wise masters themselves disparage too much knowledge, thinking and abstraction?

I decided to branch out in an attempt to avoid sinking into a hole. I worked as a Teaching Assistant in my department where I performed administrative work. I made extra money on the side by freelancing for a Korean Buddhist cultural institute within Dongguk as a Korean-English translator. I participated in a month-long traditional Korean music program for foreigners in the summer. And I took boxing lessons three times a week to sweat out the abstract toxins.

The following fall, I decided to buy a second-hand motorcycle. A maroon Hyosung Cruiser, 125cc engine with long looping handlebars, like two kitchen sink faucets on either side. This slab of metal succeeded where all of my other activities failed. It quashed my daily preoccupations about school – and the mounting irritations of living in Seoul – and brought my full attention to the present moment. I used my father's Visa card to withdraw $300 in cash and gave him some excuse about buying more textbooks. The bike set me back 600,000 won (about $600 Canadian), and I covered the other half with the money I was making as a T.A.

I was a kid again, mounting my shiny new bicycle sans training wheels for the first time. With the help of a friend, I learned to switch gears by pulling in the clutch lever with my left hand and by bumping up or down the shifter with my left foot, in one motion. I accelerated by turning the right handlebar grip toward me and braked by pressing down on the lever on the grip. Its engine rumbled with the promise of power, speed and control. If I needed to go somewhere, I could simply get up, put my helmet on and go. Once on the road, I weaved in and out of traffic and to the front of the pack, leaving tens of cars and the crowded buses in my wake as I zipped to the local TGIF's to meet the woman I started seeing. Or to Lotte Hotel's sauna and spa room for some pampering. Or to treat myself to some Hungarian salami, Brie cheese and Paris baguettes at the Hyatt Hotel deli shop up the road. Once I arrived at my destination, I could park almost anywhere, wherever there was about six feet of open space.

One afternoon, five months later, I raced out of the intersection as soon as the traffic lights turned green. Three seconds later, I heard a thunderous *Screech* to my right. I instinctively hit the brakes. I looked to my right. Staring down at me was a bulky blue truck, a few feet away, curls of smoke meandering out of its tires like an idle cigarette. I looked at the driver and he at me. We both didn't say a word. My heart was pounding. Three feet made the difference between life and death (or crippling injury). I took this as a sign and sold my bike soon after.

I decided to turn to Master Daehaeng's teachings. My mom found new life after discovering her teachings; maybe I could, too. I began to attend Master Daehaeng's Sunday Dharma Talks at the Hanmaum Zen Center in Anyang, a satellite city about an hour from downtown Seoul by subway, more often. This wasn't my first time seeing Master Daehaeng live. Nunes and I had gone to the center on occasion in my SNU days. Even before that, my entire family had an audience with her several years ago in New York, when I was a high school student. She was visiting one of her inter-national branch centers (another one of those residential homes turned Zen Center) in Flushing Meadows at the time.

I remembered my surprise at how petite and baby-faced she was (even though she was over 60 years of age) when I first met her. She sat in calm repose at the front of the room, in her humble grey robe, her head as bald as an egg. She wore a gentle smile as she observed us kneeling in front of her through her round oversized tinted glasses, as though we were a fascinating species to her. She radiated this warmth in the room that lulled my senses the way a Segovia-strung classical guitar song could, softening the pointy ends of whatever angst-ridden thoughts were preoccupying me at the time.

That experience, in turn, kindled memories of this hockey dad I once knew. I wasn't exactly sure when in my childhood this occurred. I just remembered that, after one of my hockey games, a player from the opposing team who apparently had a bad game – I think his coach benched him – came out of the dressing room with a face that said life no longer had any meaning. He was clearly sulking. Upon seeing his son, the dad gently placed his hand on his son's shoulder, leaned over and said, "It's okay, buddy. We all have bad games. You tried your best." I was taken aback. He was okay with a "bad game" and "trying your best." I had never heard this before. Master Daehaeng's silence felt like this dad's tender tap on the shoulder, as though she was reassuring me that, in the end, everything would work out.

Her Sunday Dharma Talks started at 10:30 a.m. Thousands of adherents from the surrounding areas and the eight domestic branch centers across the country would descend on the center in chartered buses, beginning as early as 8 in the morning. If you didn't arrive at least one hour before start time, it was impossible to find a brown mat to sit on inside the Main Dharma Hall, where she gave her talks. You had to stand outside between the clusters of small brick buildings of the center and listen to her via the loud speakers, weather permitting. Or stand inside the cramped main office or a private room somewhere and watch her live on a closed-circuit TV screen.

On one particular Sunday in the spring, Master Daehaeng began describing the Buddhist concept of "emptiness."

> A man was giving his wife a kiss when his son entered the room and called to him, "Daddy!" He let go of his wife and hoisted his child up, saying, "Yes, Daddy's home. Where have you been hiding?!" This time, from the other room, the man's mother called to him, "Oh, Sonny!" He put his son right down and went over to his mother. The man met three different people, and he wasn't the same each time, no? A husband at one point, a father the next, then a son the next. But which one of those identities can we say is him?
>
> What people think of as "me" or "I" is always changing and never remains the same for even an instant, so it is said that "I" is empty. Everything in our life is empty; it changes every moment.

The fluidity with which she described, in her trademark gentle voice, the man shifting from one identity to the other gave me pause. It lured forth mental images of rising and falling ocean tides. Plus, her explanation wasn't abstract and textbook rhetoric. She grounded the concept in a simple concrete and contemporary example and then gift-wrapped it in poetic prose for good measure.

The Dharma Talk and service ended two hours later. I decided not to stay for the complementary vegetarian lunch, as usual. I didn't look forward to the subsequent spilling out of people from the hall and into a very long line-up to the kitchen. I headed straight to Gwanak subway station, which was across and one block down the street.

The Seoul subway was much less crowded on Sundays, so I was able to find a seat this afternoon. I settled in for the long ride home.

Let me get this straight, I soliloquied in my head. Insofar as we wear different hats in playing different social roles throughout our lives, we have many identities. As a result, the self, the "I," cannot be defined in terms of one single and permanent identity. We wear too many hats in our lives to nail it down to THE hat. So when

Buddhism says "no self," it's not saying we don't exist physically or mentally; it's referring to the changing musical-chairs nature of our identity. "No self" equals no enduring identity that stays within us at all times, regardless of the social situation.

I drew up this social role example in my head:

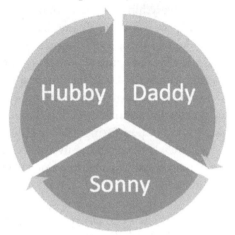

From what I could visualize, Master Daehaeng was saying there is no such thing as the "essence of me" that's firmly lodged at the core center of the above circle; my identity is entirely dependent upon the social role that I play, be it "Daddy," "Hubby," or "Sonny." The "I" merely consists of "situation-specific" pieces, like pieces of a cake. I'm not defined by one piece of the cake but the whole cake. And as the saying goes, if you're everything, then you're really nothing. I thought of that famous line from Shakespeare:

> All the world's a stage, And all the men and women merely players;
> They have their exits and their entrances, And one man in his time
> plays many parts, His acts being seven ages.

Both Master Daehaeng and Shakespeare compared life to theatre and the roles that we all play in it. And both spoke of these roles as if they were pieces of cake (as far as I could tell). The Bard of Avon, though, illustrated the seven age-specific roles we play as though each stage was a wholly different identity. Each new coming-of-age identity overthrows its predecessor, leaving the latter without a trace. The lovesick adolescent, for example, metamorphoses into the machismo adult, whose macho quality is then nowhere to be found when he becomes the mellow middle-aged professional.

Okay, fine.

But that, then, begs the question: just because I play different roles in my life doesn't necessarily mean that I, Glen Choi, don't have an underlying essence that's unchanging, does it? Master Daehaeng was only referring to the social roles we play. What about something deeper? I mean, what about the Glen during his downtime, when he's alone at home and not playing any social role in particular? That's the "true Glen." If someone asked me to describe myself, I would describe *that* Glen. I'd say that I'm … kind and caring. That is my essence, who I am. Those qualities are sewed to my soul.

This was how I saw myself in terms of Master Daehaeng's example:

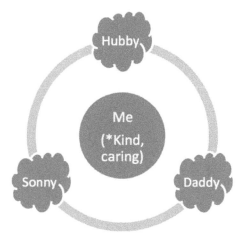

My kind and caring essence traveled with me wherever I went and whatever I did, regardless of the social role I played in a given situation – even if I acted cruel or callous, in which case it lay dormant.

I took a mental step back from the internal cross-examination. I was still puzzled. That, however, didn't bother me as much as the fact Buddhist emptiness seemed somewhat counterintuitive, not to mention unsettling. *I don't have an inner essence? But how could that be? That's like saying I don't have a soul. I mean, who says that?*

I didn't know this about Buddhism, even though I had called myself Buddhist all these years. *Embarrassing.* I had always assumed (and hoped in the back of my mind) that, at the very least, Buddhism acknowledged the existence of a permanent soul of some kind.

Whatever, I thought, yanking myself back to the present reality of the rumbling subway and the oppressive sensation of squished shoulders and standing passengers hovering over me. Solving this wouldn't exactly solve my real-life problems. As per Chongwol Sunim's advice, I put emptiness into the TBC (To Be Continued) bag and tucked this away into the recesses of my mind.

Part II
The Real World

11

Imperfect Pitch

Imagine Bob Dylan.

Imagine Dylan strumming his acoustic guitar in front of an audience as he croons about a war movie like *Saving Private Ryan*, which has the opening Omaha beach scene. Thousands of helpless U.S. soldiers are riddled with bullets as their boat vessels approach the beach. Soldiers are dying left, right and center before they even have the chance to exit their vessels.

Now let's switch it up a bit.

Imagine a Korean face (look at my photo on the back cover of this book if you're having trouble). Imagine this face decked out in a long silky white robe with a navy blue vest.

Imagine this Korean's voice sounds like Bob Dylan. *On steroids.* He stands on stage in front of an audience. He begins to narrate a story in a raspy voice. His voice suddenly roars like a lion, then soars like the piercing cry of a bat. The veins in his neck are bulging. He drops multiple octaves to growl like a wild bull. He rifles off a monotonous string of words like a rapper, then slows down to mimic the voices of ordinary folk, both women and men, young and old.

Instead of an acoustic guitar, the only instrument in the Korean's performance is a *buk*, a traditional small barrel drum, played by a drummer sitting on a bamboo mat on stage, off to the side of the singer. The drummer's left hand grips the top of a small barrel drum that stands on end. With a slender wooden stick in his right hand, the drummer slaps the leather – *slap, slappety-slap, slap*. He then taps away at the top of the drum – *tappety-tap-tap*. Then, *slap, slappety-slap, slap*. The drummer interjects "*ul-shi-gu!*" at select times to spur on the singer.

The Korean singer is animated. He raises and points a folding paper fan in a certain direction to convey great distance, extends both arms wide to reveal enormity, then flings open his paper fan to cool himself momentarily. He has no theatrical aides, no special lighting, no costumes and dramatic exits and entrances; just a folding paper fan, his limbs and his wits.

Instead of Normandy, France and WWII, time-travel almost two millennia earlier to the Far East. The Korean singer is about to wax poetic about a bloody battle that took place during the warring Three Kingdoms period of ancient China. Anarchy has prevailed among Chinese soldiers aboard their flame-engulfed wooden ship. The soldiers' spiritual faiths fail them in their dying moments. Amidst the tragedy that unfolds, however, the singer sprinkles the scene with absurdist humor, so as to corral the falling mood, to inject levity into the thick red of the subject matter:

> Some die sitting,
> Some die standing,
> Some die going,
> Some die coming.
> Some die abruptly,
> Some die because others are dying and don't want to be left out,
> Some die curious to know what dying feels like.
> All manner of death: tragic deaths, sudden deaths, instant deaths,
> death by water, death by fire, death on foreign land.
>
> One soldier, knowing he will die, beholds the nugget of poison in
> his hand.
> "It was for times like these I carried this with me."
> He puts it into his mouth and bites,
> Crunch, crunch,
> He then swallows and dies.
>
> Grabbing onto the bow of the boat, another soldier looks off into
> the distance and says,
> "O, Dragon King of the Sea,
> For the fifth consecutive generation, I am the only son in the family.
> Please, have pity and save me!"
> But he, too, dies.
>
> Another soldier staggers onto the deck only to see the expanse of the
> river water in front of him and surging flames behind him.
> Having nowhere to go, he begins his ascent up the mast.
> He claws his way up to the very top and looking in the direction of
> his home, he shouts:
> "O, Mother, my Mother! This looks like the end for me."
> He plunges into the water and dies, foam bubbles meandering their
> way to the surface.

Yet another soldier grabs onto the bow of the boat and, as he looks off into the distance,

He shouts:

"My darling, my dear darling! Woe is me that I die here, leaving behind my white-haired mother and beautiful wife." He plunges into the water.

The Red Cliff River is filled with floating bodies like loose strands of noodles in a soup.

This voice and singer make up Pansori – traditional Korean opera. And this scene is but one among a myriad in Pansori's adaptation of *The Story of the Red Cliffs*, an originally Chinese classic. *The Song of the Red Cliffs*, in turn, is one of five epics in the Pansori canon, and the themes in these epic parables run the gamut, from pure, innocent and sweet love, to valor and tragedy on the battlefield, to filial daughters coming back from the dead (yes, *The Story of Shim-Chung*, one of my childhood favorites, was among the canonized), to talking and wise animals.

It was after I watched a live Pansori performance one evening that I truly appreciated, for the first time, the meaning of the expression "Music of the Gods." I was mesmerized, enchanted and in love. I thought to myself: could I – nay, dare I – pursue a career in Pansori? Go totally off the board and sing for a living? The thought alone of a radically different career path excited me. I felt adrenaline and alive, to an extent I hadn't felt since the time I was thrust on stage during Orientation Week at SNU.

Visions of greatness danced before my eyes:

> I walk on stage in my long flowing navy blue traditional Korean robe and black horsehair top hat. In my right hand, I clutch a folding fan made of rice paper that, when unfurled, reveals the soft brush painted edges of bamboo tree branches against the grainy white background of the fan's paper.

As I clear my voice and look out into the Korean audience, I am met with hundreds of skeptical eyes: "So the kid from the West thinks he can sing Pansori, does he? We'll see about that," the eyes scream.

Undaunted, I burst into the first verse in a raw and soulful voice. The audience is stunned. I proceed to regale them with one of their beloved folk epics.

With beads of sweat streaming down the side of my face and bulging neck veins, I finally near the tenth hour of singing and the end of the epic.

I'm still gesturing wildly with my arms and fan to animate the story, sometimes falling to my knees and slapping the floor with one hand to express the crestfallen sadness of the characters. The power in my voice is all but gone, but the passion remains.

The Korean audience is moved – not only by my voice but my stamina and passion for singing and storytelling. Once I put the final exclamation point on the last lyric, I am met with a standing ovation, albeit from the three people who stayed 'til the bitter end. The Voice From The West is now the East's Favorite Son.

My singing experiences to this point consisted of singing in front of my SNU class-mates at a few of the department socials and countless times in the shower in the mornings. But I was confident that I was young (25 years old) and energetic enough to pull this off.

I promised myself I would complete my last two remaining seminar courses at Dongguk before leaving the graduate program, for good. I remembered my mantra. *Trust and believe, Glen.* Even in a worst-case scenario … even if I didn't achieve Pansori success, there had to be a reason I felt so compelled to go after this new pursuit. Maybe learning to sing in the Pansori style would … put some jam behind my voice, which was kind of feeble as it was … who knows. I imagined myself as a tree and my expe-riences the nutrients sent to my roots. The roots would expand as a result. The more experiences I had, the healthier and fuller the canopy (my character, qualities, skillset) would grow. I'd be better equipped to excel in whatever career I ended up pursuing.

I did some asking around, as well as online research. This new Internet phenome-non and the information on the World Wide Web seemed to grow by the month, and it was proving to be quite useful. I discovered that the "maestro of the maestros" of Pansori was Park Dong-Jin. Now 84, he was a living legend, recognized by the Korean government as a Human Cultural Treasure, after having sung *The Song of Heungbo* in its entirety in one sitting, for five hours straight; *The Song of the Red Cliffs* in its entirety for seven hours straight and *The Song of Chunhyang* (Korea's answer to *Romeo & Juliet*) in its entirety for eight hours straight; as well as *The Song of Shim-Chung* and *The Song of The Sea Palace.* I couldn't imagine how many people in the audience would have remained at the end. I learned that the singer in these Pansori marathons usually doesn't take a break – except for brief intermittent drinks of water, there is no official intermission – while the audience is free to come and go as they please.

Legend abounded that Maestro Park once left the secular world behind when he was younger to go off alone into the mountains to "recover" his singing voice, after it began to fade and eventually lost its luster. Desperate to fulfill his destiny as a great Pansori artist, he would practice all day long in solitude in a hut, subsisting on rice porridge, sometimes taxing his vocal chords so much he would cough up blood. At one point, he was said to have come close to dying from illness. It wasn't until his father started to bring him a folk medicinal concoction that included human feces (!) that he immediately regained his health and, ultimately, his singing voice.

Maestro Park ran a small studio in Seoul, although his prized disciple, Ms. Kim, was effectively training the next generation of Pansori singers for him due to his old age. I was warned by some of my teachers at the traditional Korean music summer program that Pansori teachers were notoriously strict and no-nonsense Old School types, which did give me pause. But I set aside my fears because the aphrodisiac of Pansori greatness was too strong to deny.

I called the studio to sign up for lessons. Ms. Kim picked up the phone. Her voice was hoarse and terse.

"We normally don't accept people who do this as a hobby," she said in Korean.

I didn't know what to say. After a short pause, her tone grew a little softer. "Are you sure you want to learn Pansori?"

"Yes …" I said like I didn't mean it. I was intimidated. I was expecting her to respond with, "Did you not hear what I just said!?"

"Then come by the studio tomorrow, and we can discuss it some more," she said.

My eyes lit up, and I felt the nourishing call of destiny again.

"Okay, thank you *very* much, Ms. Kim," I said.

The studio was located on the second floor of a tired and badly bruised building, one of many that lined this back alley of Jongno in downtown Seoul. The stairway leading to the studio was dark and dingy and squeaked loudly as I set foot on each step. *Why is a living national treasure of Korea operating out of this dive?* I thought as I carefully made my way up. It dawned on me that Maestro Park probably wasn't receiving the recognition he deserved from the general public. If he did, he could have afforded to rent or buy a newer and more upscale studio. Modern, or Western-ized, Korean music, also known as K-Pop, was all the rage in Korea. I liked it, too. But I *loved* Pansori. Its epic storylines, poignant lyrics and soulful vocals were on another level compared to K-Pop. It was the treasure of the Korean people. Koreans don't know what they're missing, I thought.

When I reached the studio doors, I could faintly hear the sound of screaming voices coming from inside, screams that oddly sounded melodious. My heart started pounding louder as I reached for the door handle. *Was I really doing this? What the hell was I getting myself into?*

I entered and realized right away I had arrived in the middle of a lesson. Ms. Kim, who was sitting on a fading maroon carpet playing accompaniment on the drums as she instructed the student, abruptly stopped the lesson.

"Please sit down over there."

The children twisted their torsos and glanced sideways at me. Their eyeballs seemed to expand in height and width as my figure became clearer, perhaps surprised to see someone older coming to learn.

"Yes, okay," I said, trying to ignore the attention.

As I sat there, I was a wide-eyed child soaking up the environment and ambience. The air was somewhat musky, reeking of antiquity. I was in awe because I was in the presence of greatness, in a studio that belonged to the great Maestro Park where I was witnessing first-hand the passing of the torch of his legendary lineage to future generations.

I panned my line of vision to dead center, where I saw three children, all elementary school-aged, solemnly sitting cross-legged on the floor, waiting for their turn to be taught by the teacher. The oldest of the bunch was the one currently being taught, and she couldn't have been more than a junior high school student. I was clearly the oldest of the students, basically double or triple everyone else's age.

The creamy clouds of awe that mushroomed in my head were suddenly punctured by Ms. Kim's voice.

"You're off tune here," she shouted at the young girl.

A few lines later: "Your voice sounds weak."

And a couple of minutes later: "Stop singing from your throat!"

To me, however, the young girl's voice was melodious and mesmerizing the whole time. I calmed myself down. Surely, I reassured myself, Ms. Kim wouldn't treat me this way when I learn; after all, I am an adult, a beginner doing this as a hobby (so she thought) and a Westerner to boot.

When the lesson ended, Ms. Kim called me over. She was a rather petite woman in her mid 30s who wore thick red-rimmed glasses that accentuated her stern countenance. Unlike her persona, however, she was kind and unassuming, albeit terse with her words, when we chatted for several minutes. I told her a little bit about my background.

"So," she said, "you came to Korea because you're interested in Korean culture. I think it's important to know your roots."

She sounded an awful lot like my mother.

"Yes, I think so," I said. "That's why I studied Buddhism at Dongguk, and now Pansori …"

We agreed I would start the following week and learn twice per week. When I returned home that evening, I couldn't help but think that Ms. Kim probably wasn't taking me seriously. Let's see how long this guy lasts, is probably what was going through her mind. Not that she gave any signs of this. But I could understand if she did feel this way because I'd probably think the same if I was in her shoes. In her eyes, I was probably some naïve Orientalist punk from the West who thought Pansori was a quaint Korean art form that wouldn't be terribly difficult to learn. Well, I wasn't and didn't, and I was going to prove her wrong.

When I entered the studio the following week for my first lesson, the little ones were all sitting cross-legged on the floor, off to the side of Ms. Kim, ready to hear me sing for the first time. I froze in terror the moment I saw them because I knew I would have to sing in front of everyone present today. I had secretly prayed almost every day for the past week that my lessons would be held in private, but apparently that's not how it was done at the studio. And they weren't about to change for my benefit. The lessons were always taught in groups, where all of the students took turns listening and learning from others' strengths and weaknesses. Man, Koreans just love to do everything in groups, I thought to myself.

The first song I was to learn was *The Song of Chunhyang*, a story about a young nobleman who falls in love with a girl named Chunhyang, who was the daughter of a retired courtesan. Their marriage was a social taboo in the old days in Korea because of the class differences, and the story regales the listener with tales of the mountains they climb in order to realize their love for each other.

Ms. Kim handed me a one-page sheet of musical notation with the lyrics typed beneath it.

"You're going to learn the first set of lyrics using this sheet."

"Yes, okay," I said, my heart beating a little stronger and body growing tenser. This was the real thing now. No more dreaming about singing or romanticizing about the storylines.

"After that," she said in rapid fire succession, "you'll be jotting down all lyrics in a separate notebook. Copy the lyrics from any one of the kids later. And get a notebook for next class."

"Yes, okay," I said.

The little girl with the pony tail opened her crinkled notebook and shoved it in front of my face to give me a preview. I noticed above and below the large handwritten words were squiggly lines that appeared to be arrows.

"By the way," Ms. Kim said, preempting my question, "you'll see there is no musical notation in the notebook."

As I later discovered, I had to learn the proper vocal register of each lyric purely through "ear memory." Ms. Kim would first sing the lyrics to me one line at a time, and I would repeat after her. I was then given time to mark down the general register of each lyric or set of lyrics (e.g. high-low-medium) by drawing approximate arrows in my notebook. It was ultimately my job to "sense" the right nuance of the register. This is how Pansori had been traditionally passed down from generation to generation. It was a completely orally based transmission. At my age and with my musical background (or lack thereof), this was also complete madness.

The first scene in the song I was to learn saw Chunhyang in prison for refusing to become one of the governor's courtesans. I placed the music sheet on a small stand in front of me that was chest-level when I sat on the floor. Ms. Kim sat facing me a couple of meters away, her drum stick in her right hand with left hand cradling the *buk*. She sang the first few lyrics. I repeated after her. I saw her cringe slightly, although she tried her best to keep a straight face. When it came time to hit the first high note, my voice cracked, and the kids burst out laughing.

"Shush! Be quiet," Ms. Kim said as she turned to face the little ones. "You guys were the same when you first started. So don't laugh."

My first one-hour lesson was unadulterated torture. I was off tune on what seemed like every single lyric and butchered all of the high notes. I burned inside with embarrassment, not only for myself but for Ms. Kim and the kids, who had to sit through the crimes and misdemeanors I was committing against their beloved Pansori. And there wasn't much I or they could do about it. I struggled to make it through the first few lines of the lyrics. By the end of the one-hour lesson, my body felt as though it had melted into a puddle, like the Wicked Witch of the West, with only the black mop of my hair on the floor.

I hopped on the bus to go home. I straddled the hanging strap in my right hand and stared out the window. Now was the time to reassess with calm and rational thought … *I was still determined*. I was going to put my head down and plow ahead. This could be my calling in life. And the lyrics and music, when sung properly, were too beautiful and compelling to give up on so soon. Moreover, I wasn't about to give up on something that even a junior high schooler – let alone elementary school kid – could do. I had some pride (really? someone might counter). If I went down, I'd go down kicking and screaming.

In between my lesson days, I often walked over to the closest mountain to my apartment, the 236-meter-high Mt. Namsan, after dinner. Seoul was home to tens of tall and small mountains, and mountains were idyllic training environments for the serious Pansori singer due to their seclusion, according to tradition. As I strolled up the winding paved roads, I would belt out the section from *The Song of Chunhyang* I had learned that week.

I invariably returned home from these nightly excursions with laryngitis and a splitting headache, thanks to a dehydrated system and all of that yelling and screaming.

One night, my mom called me after one such excursion.

"What's wrong?" she said. "What's wrong with your voice? Did something happen to you?"

"No, Omma …" I said in a raspy voice. "I told you, I'm learning Pansori these days, and I just came back from practicing at Mt. Namsan …"

"This is crazy," she said. "I don't understand what you see in it. To me, Pansori sounds like a squealing pig."

I didn't tell my dad I was going to pursue Pansori as a career. I knew he would not approve. He was under the impression it was just a hobby. My mom, on the other hand, knew that I was serious about it.

"That's because you don't appreciate its subtle beauty like I do," I said.

"You've had your fun. I'm worried about your throat and your health. Don't you think it's time you stopped now?"

"No way. I love it," I said, each word punctuated at the end with gasps of empty air. "It's such a beautiful art form."

"What a strange son I have," she said, laughing on the other end.

Mt. Namsan was known as a couples spot. Many lovebirds would park their cars along the side of the sloped roads at night for some hanky-panky. I wasn't envious, though. I was getting serious with the woman I had been seeing for a few months now. And I felt like I was serenating her each time I sang in the mountain. I did often wonder what these couples in the cars thought of me – a man wandering up the mountain roads alone at night, singing like a "squealing pig." Some cars would suddenly speed away when I neared their spots.

I became unnerved on nights when there was nary a car in sight (usually early in the week) because I was all alone in a vast darkness illuminated only by the misty yellow glow of the moon. I had watched Korean TV shows that talked about ghosts wandering the mountains of Korea, and they always seemed to pop out of the woods when the moon was at its haziest, clad in a white traditional Korean one-piece dress, their chalk-white faces accentuating the inner layer of red membrane encircling their eyelids and the darkness of their pupils. I tried to sing even louder than usual at such times, hoping that my voice would scare them off. The first set of lyrics I learned, however, didn't exactly help with this:

> Interlacing stalks of mugwort
> Does my hair resemble,
> Monster-like
> Describes my appearance

As my singing showed incremental improvement over the following weeks and months, the tone in Ms. Kim's voice turned markedly harsher, although it never approached the intensity she reached with the little ones.

"Your Korean sounds too foreigner-ish here," she said with a frown one day. I sang with an English-y, Korean-as-a-second-language accent, unfortunately.

"Yes, understood," I said.

"Okay, now louder this time," she said later.

"Okay."

"You're singing too much from the throat," she said, her voice rising but remaining steady. She pointed at her diaphragm. "As I told you, Pansori is sung from the *belly up*."

"Oh, okay," I said, cringing with guilt in front of the kids. The way she treated me was clearly softer than the way she treated them.

A month later, I came to the studio one particular day feeling battered and sans chi in my belly. I had overdone the practices in the mountain. My voice was anemic from the moment I opened my mouth. Ms. Kim sensed it, too. In the middle of the lesson, she suddenly reached back for the thick roll of toilet paper behind her and raised it above her head, poised to throw it at me.

"You can't even get past this one line!"

I was stuck trying to properly sing four words – *four words* – for about 30 minutes. My heart started racing as every ounce of my pride and self-esteem flashed before my eyes: a 25-year-old adult graduate school-educated quasi-intellectual hit in the head with a roll of toilet paper by the teacher as punishment, in the presence of his school children classmates. And yet, underneath the fear I felt a glimmer of exhilaration. It was my heart rearing its head, again.

As much as I didn't want to be treated like the kids, I wanted to be treated no different from them. I told Ms. Kim I was learning for fun so she wouldn't think I was a madman trying to become a professional Pansori singer at my age and with no musical background. I also wanted her to take it easy on me. She humored me. She held back when she taught me; not so with her young core group, at whom she often threatened to throw that same roll of toilet paper when they weren't on their game. And I was always amazed by how the kids responded. They seemed unfazed; if anything, they came back hungrier. Such a different culture here compared to Canada, I thought, amazed, the first time I witnessed this.

My plan backfired. I was the black sheep of my music family. I felt I wasn't important enough or worthy of Ms. Kim's time and effort when I observed her teach the others. I didn't commit like the kids did, in her mind that is, and only the committed merited her commitment.

Now, with Ms. Kim's right arm cocked and ready, I was just as special and worthy of her energy as the other kids. I was now a disciple my teacher cared enough about to become that incensed. It was a "welcome to the family" moment. It also reconfirmed my nagging internal conflict: while my head was attuned to health hazards, my heart was a glutton for punishment.

In the end, Ms. Kim lowered her throwing arm and calmly placed the roll of toilet paper back on the rug.

Ms. Kim called me one afternoon on my apartment landline phone. "I haven't been feeling well this week," she said in an uncharacteristic meek tone. "So for your lesson tomorrow, Teacher will be grabbing the drums for you."

By "Teacher" she meant Maestro Park, and by "grabbing the drums" she meant he'd be instructing me. My knees grew weak and my hands damp.

"Okay," I said. "I hope you're not feeling too ill."

"No, I'll be okay, thank you."

I was terrified of finally meeting the maestro himself. I winced at the prospects of seeing his aghast face once I opened my mouth. The weather was very humid today, but I decided to leave earlier than normal for Mt. Namsan, to get an early start on the practicing.

When I walked into the studio the next afternoon, sitting on the rug before me in a black necktie and white Oxford short-sleeve shirt was Maestro Park. I recognized him from his album covers, although his eyes had sunk a little deeper into their sockets, and his still-dark hair was thinning on top. He looked frail yet dignified. I noticed the little ones weren't in today. It was just him and me.

"Hello," I said, with a bow of the head.

"Hello. Please, come sit down," he said in a gentle tone, motioning me to the space on the floor in front of him with his *buk* stick. Missing from his voice was any evidence of the raw horsepower that had so captivated me, whenever I listened to a cassette tape recording of his early renditions of *The Song of the Red Cliffs*.

"What is your surname?" he asked.

"It is Choi," I said.

"And which clan are you from?"

I only knew the answer to this because of the family register document I would submit to renew my student visa.

"The Jeonju Choi Clan, sir."

He nodded his head as if to approve.

"I would like to apologize in advance but KBS will be coming today to film our lesson." The necktie and dress shirt suddenly made sense. As if meeting Maestro Park alone wasn't intimidating enough, the Korean Broadcasting System (KBS) was apparently airing a TV documentary series on contemporary Korean personalities who rose to the top of their respective fields, and Maestro Park was on their list.

"That is fine, sir," I said with a quiet gulp.

"Let us start the lesson from the beginning of the section about Chunhyang in prison." He spoke to me using honorific Korean speech this whole time. I felt awkward and embarrassed since I was so much younger and less accomplished than him. And much less wise.

I took the dog-eared brown leather notebook that I was holding in my sweaty right hand, opened it to page one and placed it on the wooden stand in front of me. I had already amassed 10 pages of scribbled lyrics to this point.

I pretended the man sitting in front of me was Ms. Kim, and I just let 'er rip like I normally would. Before long, I was almost through page one – and only once did Maestro Park interrupt to correct me. With Ms. Kim, I would have still been stuck on the first line at this point. I understood what was going on, though: at 84, he no longer had the energy to correct me on the nuances of every single note.

The KBS crew arrived toward the end of my lesson. Aside from a quick "Please, come sit down over there" by Maestro Park, I kept singing and singing, and he continued thumping and slapping away on the *buk*. We both didn't pay attention to the rolling cameras.

"Alright, let us end the lesson here," Maestro Park said.

The one hour had flown by, and the lesson went more smoothly than anticipated. As usual after a lesson, my throat felt like someone had wedged sandpaper into my vocal chords.

Maestro Park sat still and stared at me.

"You're not a bad singer," he said, pointing the *buk* stick at me, "… for a foreigner." That was, by far, the best backhanded compliment I had ever received.

Be careful what you wish for, lest it come true. This was the lesson, of another kind, that I was learning. While I may have felt acceptance and good about myself after the toilet paper incident, there was a downside. The tough love I received from Ms. Kim thereafter shifted into concerns about the acidic rebukes that were to come as I walked up the creaking dingy stairwell to the studio on lesson days.

After about four months of lessons, I began to plateau. No matter how often I practiced at Mt. Namsan, I still struggled with my vocal range, unable to hit the highest notes or nail the lowest ones (the middle register was my bread and butter).

I was never able to develop an "ear memory" for the nuanced register. In a word, I was tone-deaf. Ms. Kim would correct me by re-singing the line back to me. When I heard it again, I still couldn't figure out what I was singing wrong. To me, we sounded relatively the same (although, of course, her singing was much more clean).

I sang a lot of staccato in baritone, which sounded like someone humming in a low voice in a car that's hit a stretch of consecutive speed bumps. This seemed straightforward enough, and I thought I did a good job of it.

"It sounds forced," Ms. Kim would say, wagging her *buk* stick at me.

"It sounds weak today!" she said at the next lesson.

"It sounds throaty again," she said at the next, next lesson.

"It's too low-pitched," she said another time.

And yet on another day, "It isn't low-pitched enough!"

When it came time to hit the high notes of the song, my voice sounded like it was in the throes of puberty because it would consistently crack. I would hear the kids giggle again.

"Imagine you're singing from the top of your head," Ms. Kim once advised.

When that didn't work, she said, "Produce the sound through your nasal cavity if you have to."

When even this technique failed, she told me to just sing in falsetto, which was considered somewhat of a cop-out in Pansori.

I had trouble impersonating the various characters in the story. Pansori epics are littered with dialogue between the characters, who speak to each other in a non-singing conversational manner. In particular, I struggled with finding the voice of Chunhyang's mother.

"I see my son-in-law has come to visit," Chunhyang's mother says at one point in the story.

One day, Ms. Kim broke from her serious character after hearing my impersonation.

"Try saying that again," she said, smiling and pointing her *buk* stick skyward, "only this time elevate your pitch at the end."

I was a single twentysomething young man from the West impersonating a middle-aged mother from the East. Who was speaking to her son-in-law in that particular mother-in-law tone. I had no social or cultural frame of reference on which to draw for the "voice." I imagined I disfigured Mrs. Chunhyang in the process, transforming her into someone akin to a novice transvestite.

When I tried to time my breaths at the appropriate intervals of the song, I often ran out of air before then. Ms. Kim would then tell me to start over again from the top, after which she would inevitably find more with my singing to nitpick at than the previous go-around. At times, I worried that my singing was getting worse with time.

"What do you usually eat for your meals?" a tired Ms. Kim asked me one day after one of our lessons.

"Umm, I eat different foods like sandwiches, ramen noodles, *bab* (rice with assorted side dishes), fried chicken …"

"As the Korean proverb goes," she interrupted, "*shin-to-bul-ee.*" I knew this proverb. Literally, it meant the body and the land in which it was born are not dualistic; figuratively, it meant our genes don't lie. "We Koreans need our *bab*. You need to eat more *bab*."

My daily rice intake, or lack thereof, was apparently the source of my lackluster voice and tendency to resort to singing from my throat rather than my belly, as well as my shortness of breath.

Pansori was much more taxing on the mind and body than I could have imagined. Trying to develop a sense of the vocal registers of each lyric written down in a notebook without musical notation – except for a bunch of crude squiggly arrows – and committing pages upon pages of lyrics to memory was more mentally demanding and stressful an exercise than my school work ever was. In addition, singing from the belly to project that raw, powerful and hoarse voice unique to Pansori provided quite the workout for my abdomen.

Ms. Kim became increasingly frustrated as I continued to spin my vocal wheels. I had exhausted her energies, and she would roll her eyes and take a deep breath before scolding me again. She had grown tired of even the rebukes. The dejection that I felt at my perceived lack of improvement after several months also took its toll on my morale. I started coming to the lessons with markedly less enthusiasm and energy, first by the week, then by the day. The initial excitement of becoming the first great traditional Korean opera singer from the West lost 90 percent of its luster.

> *Maybe I simply don't have the talent, the "it" factor, to sing professionally?*
> *As with the Buddhist monastery, maybe I'm simply not cut out for this kind of stuff?*
> *Or maybe I am, indeed, too old to start now and am asking too much of myself.*

If that was the case, then that really sucked. As bad as I was, I was still madly in love with Pansori. Unlike my past pursuits, it was stimulating on multiple levels – intellectually, emotionally and even physically. But, ironically, I was currently hanging by a thread intellectually, emotionally and physically. I was headed for a nervous breakdown. I had to make a decision.

"I feel I need to take a break from our lessons," I said to Ms. Kim one day after another deflating lesson. "I'm feeling exhausted these days."

I chose my words carefully. I told myself (and her) that this would be a "temporary leave of absence," although in the back of my mind I had an inkling this would be permanent. I was too ashamed to admit to myself the possibility that I was giving up for good because that would make me a quitter. I quit when the going got a little rough. And not only once but thrice now – Pansori represented my third different career pursuit since I came to Korea.

Ms. Kim took a deep breath and gingerly leaned over the barrel of her drum in front of her.

"You do what you have to do," she said in a raspy yet motherly tone. "A break will do you good. Get some rest, and you can come back refreshed."

After a short pause, she took a moment to reflect on our time together. She spoke as though she knew this would be our last lesson.

"You did a good job here."

I was caught off guard by her comment, for two reasons. One, Ms. Kim was normally stingy with her compliments. Two, it was my impression that I had butchered *The Song of Chunhyang* beyond recognition for the last seven months.

"Really? But I had so many problems ..." I said, opening up to her more than I probably ever had with that one line.

"Everyone does," she said. "Look, you did a good job of figuring things out on your own. You might think you're a bad singer, but you're not."

12

In the Trenches

"I SEE YOU HAVE THREE BACKGROUNDS: Western, African and Korean ..." Roger deadpanned as he perused my resumé.

I burst out laughing. I was nervous heading into the interview, but his comment broke the ice.

"It's a long story," I said.

Roger was a 6'4", husky, sandy-haired American copy editor at *The Korea Herald*, an English-language national daily in Korea. He was in charge of filling the recently opened copy editor position. I sat directly across from him in the interview room, all 5'7" of me. I was a Smart car parked behind a RAM pickup truck.

I was a little awestruck by Roger, not only physically but also because he looked like the stereotypical hardened journalist that I had hitherto only seen on TV or in the movies. His tie loosely hung from his neck, his words were weighed and impeccably economical and his glazed eyes spoke to years of reporting on the front lines of the worst of humanity.

Roger, incidentally, was referring to my full name, Glen Shakwon Choi. "Shakwon" is my Korean name – sort of. My mom Anglicized "Seokwon," my properly pronounced Korean name, to "Shakwon" when an elder Jewish man who was a regular customer at my parents' corner store kept calling me "Shakwon." My mom gave up, presumed every Canadian would eventually do the same, and hence the latter name.

Roger perused the two writing samples I brought with me and, after asking me a couple of more questions, he stood up, stretched out his thick burly hand and said, "We'll be in touch."

We both got up and started walking. We passed a few work stations lined with reporters madly punching away at their keyboards, eyes glued to their computer screens.

"You know your way out?" he said.

"Yes, I do, thanks."

I waited in the fourth-floor lobby for the elevator. I heard the click of dress shoes on waxed concrete floor. I looked sideways, over my right shoulder. A couple of middle-aged Korean men wearing crisp white button-downs rolled up at the sleeve and black suit pants strolled past with their hands in their pockets. I thought about my favorite white GAP sweater, faded blue jeans and the pair of battered black Doc Martens I was wearing. I hunched my shoulders and blushed. I then glanced to my left just in time to catch the two men's side profiles disappear into the den-like space in front of the stairwell. The clatter stopped, and I heard the flicker of a lighter. A second later, creamy clouds of smoke weaved their way into the lobby.

Everyone here looks so smart and worldly.

I exited the building and into the hot and humid August air. I took a deep breath and began walking in the direction of the subway, ready to deke through the throngs of pedestrians in Myeong-dong, a trendy shopping district in Seoul. I picked up the pace so I could keep pace with the others. I let my mind wander for a moment amidst the streams of humanity flowing in both directions. I imagined myself among the throngs of Myeong-dong pedestrians again, but this time it was the next morning, and I was headed in the opposite direction. I was wearing a well-pressed dark suit, white shirt and tie, had a briefcase in one hand and the newest cellphone in the other, each step bringing me closer to the 5-storey walnut-colored building that was *The Korea Herald*. I was on my way to work.

I had applied for the position despite my lack of experience. I had once written a generic piece about the sports culture in Korea for the University of Toronto's student newspaper *The Varsity*; I wrote this the first Christmas I returned home after my freshman year at SNU (Barth wrote for *The Varsity* at the time and got me the gig). I also translated two articles from a local Korean Buddhist newspaper into English while at Dongguk. Other than that, my journalism experience was nil.

But when I stumbled upon that "Copy Editor Wanted" ad while leafing through *The Korea Herald* one day last week, a flurry of thoughts had raced through my head in that moment.

- I didn't read the paper very often and, on the off day I do, I see the job ad? What are the chances?
- I have a B.A. in English. The hiring manager would look favorably upon this. More importantly, I'd finally be putting my degree to good use.
- A journalist is supposed to be knowledgeable about a wide range of topics. I had accumulated knowledge on various aspects of Korean culture. Hence, I was a great fit as a journalist in Korea.
- So my English degree, and learning the Korean language, Buddhism and Pansori were not for naught, just as I believed.
- The pool of English native speakers in Korea is limited. My chances of being hired are very good. Great opportunity to get my foot in the door.

Maybe everything had led up to this moment, or at least this was an important step. Was I meant to be a journalist, or was I meant to acquire something important here, something that would diversify my skillset? Story-writing skills? Interviewing skills? Regardless, this in turn would serve me in some way in the end.

A few days after the interview, Roger called to offer me the job.

"Hi, Glen," Andrew said as he leaned over the low partition wall to the side of my desk. My desk was essentially the left-end section of an elongated rectangular desk that I shared with two other Political Desk reporters. "How's the story coming?"

Andrew was the copy editor of the *Weekender*, a weekly seven-page *Korea Herald* supplemental issued every Friday. Like Roger, Andrew was a big white American guy.

"Almost done," I said. "Just giving it a once-over. I'll send it to you right away."

"Alright, sounds good." Andrew knocked on the partition wall with his knuckles once, turned around and walked back to his desk.

My stomach started to churn. I loosened my tie and took off my navy blue suit jacket. It was Thursday morning, and tomorrow's edition of *The Herald* would feature my first-ever news story for the paper since I began work a few weeks ago. It would be the front-page story for the *Weekender* to be precise.

I had interviewed Hwang Byung Ki, the maestro of the *kayagum*, the traditional Korean zither, last week. He was a celebrity of sorts in Korea with his experimental and avant-garde style of music. I finished writing the final draft of the story last night, but when I came into the office this morning and saw it again with fresh eyes, I saw only dry and stiff word choices and expressions. I knew I had to spice it up, even though that's what a copy editor was for.

I started editing right away. I had time to work on it because the news stories for the Political Desk, the section to which I officially belonged as its copy editor, didn't start rolling in until the afternoon. To fill in the remaining time, my contract called for me to write part-time for the *Weekender*.

Andrew came by my desk again a half-hour later.

"So Glen ..." he said calmly, although I detected slightly more urgency in his voice now. "When do you think you can get that story to me? We're actually past the time all the stories should be in ..."

I made the decision to mentally let go in that moment. Whether or not the writing lived up to my standards didn't matter now; I had to get the damn thing in Andrew's hands right this minute.

"I'm gonna send it to your e-mail right now," I said. "Thanks, Andrew."

I turned to face my computer, saved the file, went into my *Herald* e-mail account and sent Andrew the story. As soon as I hit the "Send" button, I felt the wave of adrenaline and the air-tight pressure in my head fizzle.

Phew ... that was a close call.

We all received copies of the first print run for the Friday edition later that Thursday afternoon. Mr. Choi, the Editor-in-Chief of *The Korea Herald* (and no relation to me), called me into his office soon after. *Uh-oh*. He's probably regretting that he allowed Roger to hire me after reading my article, I thought to myself. I'd have two more strikes before I was out. My journalism career would probably end before it ever got off the ground.

I put my suit jacket back on and straightened my tie. When I stepped into his office, he peered over the paper he was reading.

"You wanted to see me, Mr. Choi?" I said, tiptoeing my way through my words. I tried to avoid eye contact as much as possible.

"Ah, Glen," he said as he put his paper down, uncrossed his legs and sat up straight on his couch. "Please, have a seat."

Mr. Choi was a stocky man in his early 50s with large penetrating eyes and wavy salt-and-pepper hair. He had studied abroad in the U.S. as a foreign student many years ago, and I detected only a slight accent to his English.

Mr. Choi leaned over, placed his elbows on his lap, crossed his fingers and released a long wheeze through his nose.

"Well, I read your story …" he said, enunciating each word as if it were his last.

I held my breath.

"And it was good."

I started to breathe again.

"I marked up a few things here and there, to tighten the writing. Overall, it was interesting."

Mr. Choi handed me the ripped page of newspaper lying on the coffee table in front of us. It was the front page of *The Weekender*, my article, with dramtic red strokes visible on it.

"Oh, thank you very much, Mr. Choi."

Going back to first grade, I had been a student for 21 years. Eight of these years I spent in university, where I was but a spectator of life, watching the world go 'round through a window, within the cozy confines of the ivory tower of academia. Pansori was a step in another direction, true, but I was still a student.

At the age of 26, my life became a full-time contact sport, for the first time. Gone was the homebody that moped, navel-gazed and pontificated, as well as the unwashed T-shirts, stretchy cotton pants, bare feet and what – in retrospect – seemed like all the time in the world. I came to work at *The Herald* every day in a crisp navy blue or dark brown suit and tie and shiny black dress shoes with matching dark-colored socks. I worked on my stories for the *Weekender* in the morning and copy edited Political Desk stories that arrived fast and furiously on my desktop in the afternoon. There were daily deadlines to meet, whether or not I was feeling it or in the mood.

No longer did I write for one person, the course professor, as in the papers I submitted as an undergrad and grad student. I wrote for the masses now, the thousands of everyday citizens who bought copies of *The Korea Herald*. They lived busy and stressful lives and had short attention spans. Moreover, they donated a portion of their hard-earned cash to read what people like me had to say. It was a privilege. But they could be a cold and demanding bunch because I had mere seconds and minutes to entertain and educate them. Time was money and, if I wasted their time, I lost their money.

Roger, Andrew and a couple of good how-to books on journalistic writing opened my eyes. The formula for grabbing and holding readers' attention, I learned, started with a catchy headline – "Hwang Byung-ki: Riding with the Legend" – followed by a witty kicker – "Kayagum master looks back on his life, forward to a busy 2001." The content then usually opened with humanizing vignettes:

> Hwang has composed and produced four albums, promptly changed the face of *kayagum* music with his avante-garde style, won eight major awards, performed in countries all over the world, and Korean poet Kim Yeong-tae has called his performances "an encounter with the supernatural."
>
> And yet for all his accolades and achievements, at first glance, there is little grandeur about Hwang: he could just as easily pass as one of those old men who play *paduk* [Korean chess] all day in Pagoda Park.

I imagined the outcome of the story had I given it an academic makeover. I might have entitled the piece "Kayagum Maestro Hwang Byung-ki: An Analysis of Selected Works." No kicker. The opening lines would read:

> Maestro Hwang Byung-ki is a contemporary scholar and performer in the field of traditional Korean music. He has composed and performed unorthodox musical works that have transcended the boundaries of the discipline. He has earned critical acclaim for such works as ...

Now imagine a reader comes across this "academic" piece at the breakfast table while sipping on coffee, just before heading off to work; or on the morning bus/subway ride to work; or on the late afternoon bus/subway ride back home, while he thinks about what to cook for dinner. I would have lost him at any point between the headline and the third line of my opening.

I also had to write more like I spoke and not like I wrote. Emotive and colloquial expressions were the new mantra. Hwang didn't develop an unusual interest in the *kayagum*, he *fell in love* with it; Korean audiences didn't undervalue his music, they didn't know what *all the fuss* was about.

The job wasn't without its pressures, but if I wrote a great story, its potential positive impact on thousands of people made the pressure well worth it.

My 2 *million* won (about $2,000 Canadian) monthly salary also made it worthwhile. It cut me loose from the shackles of financial dependency. No longer would

I feel a twinge of guilt every time I splurged or indulged because any money wasted hereafter would not be my father's but my own.

"Hi, everyone," I said in English, clasping my hands.

I was sitting on the creamy white *jangpan-ji*–sheeted floor at a restaurant with the rest of the Political Desk team. It was Friday night, and I was at another *hwe-shik*, or team dinner. There were eight of us at the table, all native Koreans who were reporters for the Political Desk, except for Jon and me. Jon was the other Political Desk copy editor, a fellow Canadian from Montreal. Like Roger and Andrew, he was a big strapping 6'2" white guy. *The Herald* would have made one formidable football team had there been an intercorporate football league.

We were going around the table to say a few words about our experiences at work thus far. The restaurant was packed and buzzing with chatter. Our middle-aged waitress speed-walked back and forth to bring over our food. She first brought over a bevy of spicy and pickled vegetable side dishes that she put at the center of the table, followed by our individual metal bowls of steamed rice and finally the main course: large leafs of romaine lettuce and *samgyubsal,* raw and fatty slices of pork belly meat, which we all waited – with the tips of our chopsticks in our mouths – to slap onto the in-table grill that was warming up.

I had already downed a strong alcoholic drink and was feeling a nice warm tingling sensation in my face and hands.

"As you all know," I continued, "I've only been working at *The Herald* for about a month now. But I'm enjoying it and learning a lot. You've all been very nice, helping me along the way, especially Jon."

I looked to my left and saw Jon smiling.

"I hope my copy editing is helping," I said, turning to the rest of the reporters with a smile, "and if you have any questions, please ask me anytime."

I was giving a mini-speech in English for essentially the first time, at the urging of Mr. Lee, the head of the Political Desk, who thought he was helping me since English was my first language and everyone present spoke excellent English. I actually felt more awkward, kind of like when I opened my mouth for the first time after having my braces removed when I was 12.

"Anyway, I'm very happy to be part of the Political Desk team, and I look forward to getting to know everyone better in the future. I will do my best to contribute to the team."

The others lightly clapped.

The awkwardness I felt was tempered by the fact I had done enough of these speeches in the past – including at Dongguk, albeit less so – that I subconsciously followed a generic template. In the end, it was a matter of fleshing it out: *break in the audience with a line or two about the past > humbly deflect any current personal accomplishments to the group or team effort > end warm and fuzzy with one or two lines of expressed hopes for the future.* I probably sounded like a polished politician giving his election-night victory speech, that is, highly scripted with a vague promise to do something at the end.

Saying a few words at a social gathering in Korea was like a national pastime. Whether I was at a gathering of fresh-faced and giddy undergrads or world-weary and hardened journalists. But there was one marked difference between these two groups when it came to socials: alcohol. Journalists drank a lot more of it. That was only natural, since tight deadlines could make for some frayed nerves and tension between co-workers or superiors and subordinates, and alcohol was the panacea that took some of the edge off.

It was at the team dinners that I first learned of the boilermaker, a shot glass filled with either *soju* (rice liquor) or whiskey that is then dropped inside a glass of beer. We began drinking the boilermakers even before our meals came out. Once one person downed his or her glass in "one shot," mixed Korean-English lingo – "Konglish" – for "in one chug," his duties weren't done. He next had to pass the empty glass to the person sitting beside him and then pour the beer in the glass and whiskey in the shot glass for that person who, in turn, received each with two hands. Giving and receiving with both hands was considered a show of deep respect for your fellow human being. We drank in turns like this, going around the table.

I got the impression that the boilermaker was one of those tacit Korean codes that, if violated, led to ostracization. Either way, I didn't care. If it gave me and those around me a good buzz, I was going to partake.

The air turned into a smoky mist. The greasy slices of pork were now sizzling and ripe for the taking. I picked up the juiciest piece I could find from the grill with my chopsticks, placed it on a dewy lucent green leaf of lettuce spread out over my left hand and used my chopsticks again to garnish the piece of meat with a clove of garlic and some spicy red pepper paste and sesame oil. I promptly stuffed the lettuce wrap into my mouth. *Umm-mm.* Heaven. The pre-meal buzz seemed to enhance the taste.

It was time for round two of the boilermakers. From person to person it went, until the suit jackets and ties came off completely, rosy cheeks bloomed and the smiles and laughter came out from hiding behind steely faces.

I felt someone patting me gently on the blade of my right shoulder. I looked to my right. It was Mr. Jung, a slender man probably in his late 40s and a veteran writer of *The Herald*. He was looking at me down his nose with head slightly tilted back but with a smile, as if to say, "You're alright for a new guy."

I smiled back. I was pleasantly surprised.

Mr. Jung wasn't friendly when I first met him at the office. He was cold and distant and didn't talk to me. I thought to myself, "Probably thinks I'm some entitled punk who parachuted in, landing the job at *The Herald* only because I'm a native English speaker, who didn't have to pay his dues and was without the proper qualifications." And if that's what he thought ... well, he was right. Meanwhile, he probably rose up through *The Herald* ranks one word, article and year at a time.

The team dinners seemed to open him up more. It was as though my willingness to "throw back a few" altered his perspective and made me a good guy in his eyes. The fact that I drank signaled to him that I was willing to let go and be vulnerable and was open to making a fool of myself in front of others. I had basically earned some of his trust. Alcohol was the great equalizer.

"Does anyone have anything else to say?" Mr. Lee said after we were all but finished eating.

"Maybe something you're dissatisfied with at work, or how we can make the Political Desk better?"

I was again pleasantly surprised. This time by Mr. Lee and his rather democratic attitude, which belied his beady brooding eyes that were magnified by his thick black-rimmed glasses and his stern clenched countenance at work. I originally pegged him as the archetypal top-down authoritarian boss.

Silence.

Mr. Jung then ahem-ed us. I heard some serious phlegm come up in the process. He was about to speak up. As the elder statesman among the reporters at the table, he had earned his stripes to do so. On the other hand, a younger or junior-level employee   pretty much everyone else at the table tonight – who openly critiqued or questioned the decisions by the "higher-ups" – the more senior, seasoned and thus wiser amongst us – could be interpreted as acting disrespectfully or arrogantly. If any of us younger folks were going to say anything, it had better be worded carefully and diplomatically, and said after Mr. Jung, who had the floor first.

"Well, ahem," Mr. Jung began, "in my opinion …"

I tuned him out as soon as he opened his mouth. My Spidey senses told me we were entering the "each person must sing a song for us" territory, and I wanted to think about which Korean pop song I recently learned to sing. Thinking about Pansori was off-limits; the lyrics and plaintive vocals were too heavy and intense for the situation.

"Okay, thank you," Mr. Lee said several minutes later. "That is a good point, and we should try to make our operations more efficient in that respect."

As if on cue, Mr. Lee then broke into a mischievous grin and asked, "Now does anybody have a joke to share, or a song to sing … ?"

Silence again.

A joke? Hmm, that was something different.

"Well, I have a joke to tell," I said.

"Good," he said, breaking into an even wider grin.

I was buoyed by the fact my repertoire of jokes had increased by two since my SNU days, and I wanted to get them off my chest.

The room turned silent. I could sense anticipation underneath the glazed eyes of my colleagues. They were eager to listen because of the promise of laughter in the end. I was both intimidated and excited by the challenge.

"A Korean student studying overseas in the U.S. is caught one day for driving over the speed limit by a policeman …" I said.

"When the policeman walks over to the car, the Korean student rolls down his window and says, 'Please, close your eyes.'" (Which is the literal Korean equivalent of the English idiom "to look the other way.")

A round of chuckles.

The joke wasn't over.

"So what do you think the American policeman said to the student?" I said to everyone.

"I don't know," some of them murmured.

"No soup." (Which is the literal Korean equivalent of the English expression "not a chance.")

The laughter was heartier than when I told the first part of the joke. The absurdist line in the end must have given the joke just the right amount of sandpaper it needed.

As the night wore on, I became intoxicated. It wasn't just the alcohol talking. It wasn't simply the exhilaration of performing for an audience. It was more than that. The speeches, the jokes, the drinks, the silliness, these were but fodder for a campfire over which we – strangers who came in from different parts of the cold – crowded together to warm our hands and bond.

We went out for team dinners almost every week. I crashed the Business Desk *hwe-shiks* from time to time. I was enjoying myself. I loved bonding with as many of my Korean colleagues as possible. On nights we were all feeling it and having too good a time to call it a night (which meant just about every team dinner), we would put our smoke-drenched suit jackets back on and move to round two of the partying (which meant karaoke). By the time we called it a night, it was usually 1 or 2 a.m., and I would have to take a taxi home because the subway had closed.

As the dinner socials induced a sense of belonging at *The Herald*, I felt one with the 50 million people of South Korea when riding in those Hyundai sedan taxis. Korean cabdrivers loved to gab, and they sought my two cents on whatever issue was bothering them that evening, which was usually one of three things: all that's corrupt with current Korean politics (their personal favorite), the loss of traditional values among the younger generation of Koreans today or the unpredictable weather.

In my first few years in Korea, the cabbies knew I wasn't from these parts after only a couple of sentences out of my mouth. During my M.A. years, however, I was able to increase the sentence count to around 10-to-15 before they flashed their trademark bewildered expression and said, "Where are you from?" or, "You're not Korean, are you? You look it, but you don't sound like it." Their incredulous tone made me feel like some interplanetary visitor, not just someone from another country.

The questions had now stopped. I had the Korean accent and intonation down pat. The once jumbled and "nomadic" Korean pronouns, nouns and verbs settled nicely in my head and, when called upon, took their rightful places swiftly and without complaint: verbs to the end of the line, subjects (when required) to the front, objects to the middle. The muscles in my mouth required to clearly enunciate sounds foreign to the English language had also become leaner, crisper and more agile. In a word, I had become fluent in Korean.

So I now looked the part, talked the part and walked the part. The trifecta was complete, and I was no longer *other*, a *kyopo*. I had finally lived up to my Korean name, Shakwon. My mouth would curl up into a smile every time I exited the taxis. The tightly wound ball of memories of my outsider status would unravel, string by string, each time this occurred.

"Hey, Albert, how's it going?" I said as I strolled up to his desk with both hands in my pockets.

It was Monday morning, the weekend after my story on the Korean folk song *Arirang* was published. It was my third feature story since I became the full-time copy editor for the *Weekender*. Andrew had recently left for greener pastures, and I was asked to take over for him.

"Busy copyediting – you know the drill," Albert said, straining his neck from side to side and twitching his nose, something he seemed to do quite often, as if a nervous tic. "I gotta get on the story I promised you for the next *Weekender*."

Albert was like the little brother I wanted to take under my wing but never had. He was six years my junior and had recently come to Korea, both to further his journalistic aspirations as well as re-connect with his heritage. Like me, his brand was Korean, but he was manufactured entirely in North America, the U.S. in his case. As his *sunbae* of sorts, I wanted to show him the Korean ropes.

"Yeah, okay, sounds good," I said. "Let me know if there's any Korean stuff you need me to translate into English for your story."

"Sure, will do," he said in his soothing baritone voice, which belied his tall, pencil-thin frame.

I opened with small talk as segue to what I really wanted to talk about.

"By the way, just wondering if you ever read my story on *Arirang* …" I said as I turned back around to face him after feigning one step toward my desk.

"Yeah, it was good," Albert said.

"Oh, thanks …" I said, waiting for the gushing to start at any moment.

"… … … …"

"… Alrighty," I said, "so look forward to seeing your story when you're done."

"Okie-dokie."

I returned to my desk and started to type up a list of contributing writers for the upcoming edition of the *Weekender*. My fingers felt heavy on the keyboard. Clunk, clunk, clunk.

It wasn't long before I heard the familiar rumble of rolling wheels and the wonky squeak of an office chair. I looked over to my right to see someone two rows down standing up from his desk. It was a Business Desk reporter getting up to leave. He slid both his hands in his pant pockets and made his way to the elevator lobby, walking with purpose and an ever-quickening pace, his gaze straight and narrow. Probably adrenaline before the deadline, going for a smoke to blow off some steam.

A couple of minutes later, another rumble and wonky squeak, but from the far end of the newsroom this time. It was Yong-Hee, my former colleague at the Political Desk. She marched over to the head of her row where sat Mr. Lee. Her mouth moved to enunciate a few short words to him, to which he nodded his head in agreement without ever taking his eyes off the computer screen. *Probably announcing to the boss she just submitted her article for today.* Yong-Hee had a noticeable spring in her step and smile on her face as she walked back to her seat.

This played like a broken record throughout the day: the rumbling of the wheels, the squeak of the chair and another rising body, until these people became like a streaming blur of black and white lines in front of me. Such moments had increased with alarming frequency over the past three months. Reporters moving with purpose and passing by me. Story ideas flowed through their fingertips and onto their keyboards, lifted them from their chairs and propelled them forward to their editors with proposals. Their ideas crossed disciplines, time periods and cultures.

My Western colleagues at *The Herald* – a hodgepodge of expats that included white Americans (Roger, Burke), Korean-Americans (Albert, Mi-hui), a Scotsman (Peter), Kiwi (another Peter), white Canadian (Jonathan) and an Australian (Ben) – were no exception. They wrote about the international rise of the Korean film industry; a former Korean Special Forces guy teaching martial arts in the U.S.; the growing underground Korean punk music scene; the Korean animation team responsible for drawing The Simpsons; and the best watering holes in Seoul.

Or they crossed over into more serious news pieces about foreign workers' human rights issues in South Korea, American NGOs and North Korea relations, and South Korea in the global economy.

Meanwhile, back at the ranch, I would hold on tight to my teddy bear known as Traditional Korean Culture. I didn't feel like holding anybody else because Traditional Korean Culture was the only topic that comforted me. In fact, I thought it deserved longer and richer essay-esque pieces than the short and somewhat superficial treatment I gave it in my articles. Then again, that probably wouldn't have sat well with my readers, who were mostly expats who worked full-time in Korea (usually teaching ESL).

They wanted to unwind heading into the weekend. They wanted to read about off-the-beaten-track adventures and travel spots in Seoul and other regions of Korea. About eateries and cafés considered hidden gems. Foreigner-friendly watering holes and sporting activities. Not about the history of the Korean folk song *Arirang* or the traditional Korean spring festival known as *Dano* or the history of the Korean Buddhist monastery called Songgwang-sa. The fact that my personal e-mail Inbox at *The Herald* remained dead silent in the days following the publication of one of my stories kept reminding me of this. My brain understood, but my heart didn't want to follow through.

I washed away my feelings of impostor guilt with boilermakers, soju and pints of Korean lager at *The Herald's* dinner socials. After some time, this, too, got old and unsatisfying. It became a drag to booze in the evenings to relieve the tension, only to wake up the next morning with a nasty hangover and a sobering emptiness that killed any motivation to do work that day. It was counterproductive, a self-defeating cycle.

Then something unexpected broke the cycle, bringing my mom to visit. I hadn't seen her for two years. Her boyish short hair and the entrenched creases between her eyes were as familiar to me as the morning sun. But the hesitation in her step and the jerkiness of her movements today – and the past week, for that matter – were disorienting.

The mom I knew, based on the first 18 years of my life, slid her feet across the oat-beige carpet of 524 Eglinton Ave. W. as she glided from kitchen to dining room to laundry room. She went out every day during the week to work and on weekends to shop. She was so sure of herself and her abilities when she conducted her business.

Here, in her younger brother's apartment in Yeouido district in Seoul, my mom sat for most of the day on the yellow oiled-paper flooring in a small rectangular room. When she ventured into the kitchen, she would first pause before remembering which drawer contained the chopsticks and spoons, or which cabinet to find the pots and pans. She fumbled with the buttons on the laundry machine and the TV remote controller in the living room. The rare times she did go out, she wore a surgical mask because she felt discomfort in her throat whenever she breathed. She would squint her eyes at the subway map I showed her, trying to square in her head the zigzag of lines. She was quick to tire of the relentless waves of pedestrian traffic and wanted to return home as soon as possible. She looked in turns timid, awkward, displaced and lost – without a mental nest in which her past identities could rest. Amazing what context does to our perception of others, I thought.

She was lost in another sense. Time, in the form of almost three decades, had industrialized and modernized Seoul beyond recognition. Skyscrapers, smaller commercial and apartment buildings, Christian churches and paved streets had sprouted over the open fields of grass she once roamed with her friends. The motherland my mom so loved no longer existed, except in memory.

I asked her if she still wanted to move back one day.

"Yes, of course," she said with some growl behind her voice. "But ... to the countryside, where the air is better."

My mom turned her head away from me. The wrinkle lines between her eyebrows squished up against each other, and her lips pursed like a fish. She pressed down with both her arms as though she was kneading flour. She began to massage the left thigh of the person who was there the whole time lying down before her, a person who lay still and silent on the creamy white *yo*. My mom's hands then hopped down the shin, back up the thigh, then further up the waist, left shoulder and along the arm.

"What are you doing?" I said in a lowered voice.

"I'm trying to help your grandmother get back strength to her left side." She was still quite warm there, my mom said, even though the doctor had diagnosed her with paralysis to the entire left side of her body. Warmth meant blood was still flowing, which in turn meant there was hope for the feeling and movement to return one day. So my mom rationalized.

Grandma had become an invalid. It happened on the family farm in Paju, an hour and a half's drive southeast of Seoul, where she stepped out into the frigid December cold to shovel the snow one morning when all of a sudden a cold draft burst a blood vessel in her brain and paralyzed one side of her body. She was in grave condition, unable to enunciate or walk for the most part. My mom took the earliest possible flight out of Toronto to be by her mother's side.

The news shocked me. Even at the age of 88, with the exception of some aches and pains to her fingers and knee joints, Grandma had been in excellent health. She was living with her son and his family in Seoul when I first arrived from Canada and stayed with them for a few months. Up until only a year ago, before her move from the city, every Sunday she would bus it alone to the morning Buddhist service at Chogye-sa Temple in Jongno. During the day, she would disappear into her room, sit on the floor in the corner and recite the Thousand Hands Sutra or the Diamond Sutra in whispers, while rocking her small and round figure back and forth.

She would help my aunt prepare the meals, do the dishes and keep all corners of the apartment tidy. She often bolted out of her seat on the couch in the middle of an afternoon TV show because she had just remembered another chore on her mental to-do list. One of her greatest fears, she once confided to me, was that she'd outstay her welcome, unable to contribute to the family in some practical way due to her old age or, worse, force others to nurse her and hence be reduced to something of a nuisance to her children and grandchildren. Living a long time, she warned me, was more of a curse than a blessing. She owned very few possessions: a few tops and dresses that neatly fit into one medium-sized bag, a hairpin and a coat. She was mobile at a moment's notice. It was as if she wanted to ensure her children wouldn't have to labor through her belongings if and when she passed on.

My fondest memories of her occurred at the breakfast table. She would some-times plop a second fried egg on top of my bowl of white steamed rice once I finished the first one. When I would look up at her with a frown (I was getting full), she would wave her hand and, with a few scornful blinks of her eyes, shush me with, "Just hurry up and eat it. You're still a growing young man." She reminded me of my mom, always trying to make me fatter. In Korean culture, looking fatter meant you looked healthier. I assumed this had something to do with the stinging and lasting memory of rampant poverty in Korea's recent past, around the time of the Korean War, and the fact that thinness of body was associated with this harsh time. I would sometimes mock my grandmother by encouraging *her* to "eat up," to which she would let out a short staccato of whimpers that was her version of a hearty laugh.

"I had a dream last night," my mom said as she laid her arms down to her side, her voice growing incredulous. "One of the adherents at the Toronto Hanmaum Zen Center kept pleading with me to sit down where I was so she could properly honor me with a prostration. I was dumbfounded. And embarrassed. I mean, what did I do to deserve such an honor?"

My mom insisted to her fellow temple-goer this was preposterous, but her friend persisted.

"So I finally agreed but only on the condition that we both prostrate to each other, as equals and both worthy of this honor, and she agreed. So I went down to the ground to prostrate ..."

Pause.

"But as soon as I looked up ... my friend's face had turned into your grandmother's." My mom let out a grunt of disbelief.

"Grandmother looked at me and laughed rather sheepishly. I was so taken aback I woke up ... It was all so vivid."

According to my mom, while Grandma couldn't speak, her face had always spoken of a yearning to tell her something. She now knew. Grandma had wanted to express her gratitude, grateful that my mom had come all the way from Canada to be by her side. So she did this through her dream, borrowing a more likely face because she knew my mom would never dare accept a prostration from her own mother.

I sensed my body was ready to shut down for the night. "Omma, I should go home now. I have work tomorrow." It was approaching 9 p.m., and the apartment I shared with Burke, my colleague from *The Korea Herald*, was a good 40-minute bus and subway ride away.

"Yes, yes, by all means. You should get some rest." I could tell she felt bad I had a long ride home.

"Oh, and thank you, my son," she added.

"For what?"

"For being here for your grandmother." My mom's tone was at once pleased and melancholy. "I'm sure your grandmother is touched that you are here."

"I just hope my being here lifts her spirits a bit. I'll come to visit again this week. Call me on my hand phone if there's an emergency."

I kneeled over my grandmother, who looked up at me with a pale face and helpless and longing eyes, like a muzzled hostage trying to plead for clemency.

"I'll come back soon to visit again, Grandma," I said in a louder-than-usual voice.

I slid my right arm through my walnut-colored suit jacket and tugged at the collar. "Please take care and rest ... By the way, how handsome do I look in my suit?"

I had hoped to hear that familiar whimper-laugh, but her face remained stoic and devoid of the life with which it once teemed. My spirits sagged to the floor in that instant. Grandma was one of the good ones and didn't deserve this. Yes, she lived a long life, but she deserved a peaceful end. And she was almost there. She was through and through a hardworking, conscientious, kind and selfless person. *Of all the people, why her?* Elderly people withstand sudden exposure to cold drafts every day, I thought. Buddhism would probably say that fateful moment was the ripening of conditions for dormant karma from past lives to manifest itself. Well, if that was true, I wanted to see with my own eyes exactly what she did in her past to merit this suffering. In this case, I couldn't just believe such an explanation.

I picked myself up, waved good night to my mom and, as I closed the room door behind me, I could only hope that, somewhere underneath her pale exterior, Grandma had managed a smile at my earlier comment.

My grandmother's chest and neck curled upward as she heaved one last breath. It caught everyone in the room by surprise. We thought the gasp of air she let out several moments ago was her last. We waited ... and waited. No breath came. My uncle grabbed his mother's hand and cried, "Mother!" My mom leaned forward, wrapped both her hands around the face of Grandma, whose eyes were shut, and cried, "O Mother! ... Mother! O Mother!" My aunt, my three cousins and I kneeled behind them in silence with heads bowed. Tae-nyung, one of my cousins who was a medical doctor, got up to check my grandmother's pulse one last time. There was none.

As the son and hence patriarch of the family, my uncle would decide on what would happen to my grandmother's corpse. He had planned to bury her body together with my grandfather's in his tomb, as was the tradition in Korea, as well as Grandma's request. My mom wasn't at all comfortable with this idea. Cremation was the Buddhist way. Besides, she thought, digging up grandfather's coffin was a costly and inefficient process. She visited Anyang the very next day to consult with Master Daehaeng, who suggested a compromise – cremate the body and sprinkle the ashes around grandfather's grave, in a sort of hybrid traditional Korean-Buddhist co-burial rite. Master Daehaeng had mentioned that was the original spirit behind the traditional idea of co-burials anyway. She also instructed my mom to bring a portion of the ashes to the temple, where the monks would go and sprinkle it in pure and pristine river water deep within the valleys of Korea. As a Buddhist himself, my uncle agreed to the idea.

Something else gnawed away at my mom's conscience. Grandma had grown up without a father, who had gambled away his earnings and left the family almost destitute. Grandma's mom divorced him early in the marriage as a result, which was a social taboo of the highest order at the time, and she and her mother had become social pariahs in their village. Then Grandma's mom, apparently a very attractive lady, caught the eye of a wealthy local government official, with whom she later re-married. The man did not allow Grandma to live in the same house, probably because of the vicious rumors that would circulate in the small community if she did. So Grandma lived with her grandmother, who had become a Buddhist nun and lived alone in a small house she had built.

This nun was quite the disciplinarian with her and her cousin, who also lived with them. The nun saw that Grandma was fair and very pretty and feared that the village men might take a fancy to her. In traditional Korean Confucian culture, it was forbidden for girls and boys even to sit together beginning at the age of seven. So the nun only allowed the cousin to wear all of the pretty silk clothes that Grandma's mom would bring as gifts when she visited, and only the cousin was allowed to attend school and receive an education. The nun also married off Grandma when she was 16 to a man in the village, a local farmhand who was 35, poor and single. This was the nun's way of helping out those in the village who were less fortunate. Grandma's mom protested but, with tears streaming down her face, Grandma reassured her that she would live a happy life with her new husband. The story kind of sounded like the real life Korean-village version of the Cinderella tale … without the happy ending.

My mom, however, was determined to tie her mother's tale with the elusive ribbon and bow. She was ridden with guilt because she was never able to truly spoil her mother, who had been a gentle and loving soul despite her past. This was now her last chance. And she knew what it was she had to do. She was going to purchase one of the Pagodas for the Spirits of the Dead at Gwangmyung Zen Center. There would Grandma – her name enshrined on memorial tablet paper contained inside a white clay jar, which, in turn, was encased inside the pagoda – receive the care she so deserved. The resident monks would routinely cut the grass surrounding the tens of pagodas in the park, sweep off any debris and perform memorial services for these spirits. The last service was especially vital since many spirits believed they still lived in this world in their previous physical forms, when only consciousness remained. They needed to be reminded as often as possible to let go of their bodies so they could move on to the next life.

My mom called my father. She needed his approval to use their joint-account Visa card to purchase not one but two of the pagodas. One of each for both the Jung and Choi family clans. Desires followed the dead, and the ancestral spirits on my father's side would become covetous if only the maternal side of the family owned one. The pagodas, produced from marble, did not come cheap. My father was, at first, flabbergasted. Christmas season was the busiest time of the year at the post office, and he had to cover for my mom while she was here, and now she was demanding more money! Despite the fact he wasn't very religious himself and quite skeptical about the afterlife, my father said yes. My mom mused this was his way of thanking her for the years she nursed his father, my paternal grandfather, when he lived with them in Toronto a few years ago, before his death. When I visited Toronto during my winter breaks, I remembered seeing my mom assist my grandfather with his urinary and bowel needs.

My mom and I bussed it down to Gwangmyung Zen Center, my old stomping grounds. When we arrived, the time I spent with Chongwol Sunim, with whom I still kept in touch, came to mind. I remembered how homesick I felt at the time. I smiled. Painful experiences in the rear view mirror were rosier than they appeared in the present. Sunim had long since moved on, now stationed at a temple near the southern tip of the Korean peninsula, where he was furthering his studies in the Vinaya, the rules of ethical conduct for Buddhist monks.

The funeral service commenced inside the Main Dharma Hall. The presiding monk beat the *moktak* at a steady pace as he chanted the Thousand Hands Sutra. I scanned the altar. Six objects were spread across, each designed to soothe and comfort the spirits of the dead present (other spirits supposedly converged whenever such a service was performed): a clay bowl full of clean water … which cleanses any of the Five Desires that arises from contact between the five senses and external objects (these desires sullied the mind); a large round white rice cake … to convey the idea of the circular oneness – the interconnected nature of the past, present and future – that is reflected in the very self; burning incense sticks … representing the sweet scent of incense inherent in the heart, which then never goes hungry; candles … a reminder of the light within, which melts away the ignorant mind and body in the way it does the wax candle; vases of flowers and a plate of fruit (when one's mind evolves and flowers, one bears its fruit).

The monk concluded the service with a chant of the *Musang-gye*, or "The Principle of Transience":

Dear Spirit, since such is the cycle of life, that thy strands of hair, fingernails,
    teeth, and thy hide, skin, tendons, bones,
that this physical body that is like dead skin cells all eventually return to
    the earth,
and things such as saliva and nasal discharge, pus, blood, bodily fluids,
    phlegm, tears, vital energy and urine all return to water,
the body's hot energy returns to fire,
the energy from activity transforms into wind,
since the Four Elements of the body each disperse back to earth, water, fire,
    wind, their respective places,
where, today, can we find Spirit's body that has but returned to the
    elements …

The words, every line, in this particular verse grabbed my attention by the throat. They were raw, naked, intense. A chill shot up my spine.

We put on our coats to move outside, to the immediate left of the Main Dharma Hall building. My mom and I stood side by side with bowed heads, hunched shoulders and bare hands clasped together at our chest. The icy wind nipped away at our reddened cheeks. Beneath our black dress shoes lay sticky clumps of brown-white slush. The monk from the service, now clad in a grey fur hat, took the piece of paper on which my grandmother's name was handwritten in Korean calligraphy, lit it over a flickering candlelight and placed it inside the belly of the miniature stone pagoda in front of him. We watched in silence as the fire devoured the paper. He reached over to grab a handful of the ashes with his bare hand, the pieces he missed fluttering about in all directions. The latter was intentional, to signify the flapping away of the consciousness of the dead, which had been freed from its physical shackles. The monk sprinkled the ashes over a separate clay bowl full of clean water and walked over to a nearby tree, around the base of which he gently poured the water.

We followed the monk down the paved path, one that I had taken countless times for a stroll when I stayed here. We stepped onto the grassy field that sparkled with snowflakes. The tails of our long coats flapped in the wind as we walked past a line of life-sized rock towers. In the middle of the row stood the Jung clan pagoda. It was a thick and impenetrable slab of grey marble, multiple-tiered with a crown-like spire at the very top, a hat-like eave below it, a pentagonal midriff that featured carvings of the swastika – an ancient and deeply auspicious symbol in Buddhism – and the Buddha sitting in meditative repose, and a flowering lotus at the base. The monk opened a small door at the structure's square foundation and, one by one, inserted the several white clay jars that had been sitting next to the foundation when we arrived. Each jar had an individual name inscribed on it, including names from two generations and one generation above my grandmother's (her grandparents and parents, respectively), along with one with my grandmother's and another with my grandfather's name. When it came time for my uncle and aunt to go in, the jars for my great great grandmother's generation would be cycled out in a ceremony. Three successive generations of ancestors in one pagoda at any one time, this was the policy. We walked up a few flights of steps on the side of the hill to an upper-level tier, where the Choi clan pagoda was ensconced among others. The monk inserted jars on which were inscribed the names of my paternal great great grandparents, great grandparents and grandparents. My parents and then my sisters and I would follow suit.

I felt a pricking in the back of my head. With a furtive glance I looked up. The Choi clan pagoda gazed straight at me, still and stone faced. It didn't blink. *Your teeth, your fingernails … decay to dust*, it echoed. *Your actions become air*, it echoed. And echoed. Me. My mom. My father. My sisters. People I loved, people I wanted to make happy, people who would vanish in the end, as would our accomplishments. Existential doubt suddenly crept into my head. What was all this for, anyway? All of this running around and chasing after something, my dreams and my future – as if I was trying to pick a mushroom that, upon second look, was but a cloud.

I graduated from Dongguk University one and a half years later. I was working as a PT copy editor for the online English edition of *The Chosun Ilbo* after leaving *The Herald*, where I had completed my one-year contract. It was then that I decided to get my act together. I would use my free time to complete my Master's thesis. It was the last thing that stood between me and a graduate degree, and I didn't want a half-baked degree rotting in the back of my head for the rest of my life.

When I re-connected with my thesis supervisor (who joked I had gone AWOL), he told me I could write the thesis in English, which only further fueled my desire to finish. I didn't hem and haw over the thesis topic. I would write about the role that Western psychology played in the transmission of Buddhism in the West. This was the one course topic back in the day to which I could relate: the course focused on some of the cultural-psychological differences between East and West, which clicked with both my experiences growing up in Canada and living in Korea. The Eastern self, said psychotherapist Mark Epstein in *Thoughts Without a Thinker*, was "enmeshed" in a web of family, hierarchy and group expectations. The Western self, on the other hand, was an "estranged" one that was more autonomous, yes, but also more prone to feelings of alienation and isolation. These opposite starting points necessitated the intervention of Western psychological techniques in the transmission process. The more I reflected, the more I realized this was a fascinating argument. It never occurred to me that the Buddhist tradition and its practices might not be "complete" as is, that different cultures had unique wants and needs that rendered religious traditions fluid.

I buried myself in books, journal articles and writing. When I was struck with writer's block or lost interest, which occurred from time to time, I plowed ahead. *Boo-hoo*. No excuses, I thought. I finished the 70-page thesis in a year.

I moved on to work for one other media outlet in Seoul before I made The Decision. It was time to move on. Not only would I leave journalism for good, it was time to go home to Canada for good.

I loved Korea. It felt like home. I was fluent in the language. I had built a wide social network of friends, colleagues and acquaintances. Other than my family and relatives, I knew no one in Toronto. Even with the recent advent of e-mail, my communications with Barth, who had moved to New York many years ago to pursue a career in journalism, had grown fewer and far between in the convening years. It was only a matter of time before he would become the latest – and last – Toronto-friend casualty. My luck with women had changed here, too. I almost got married to a talented and gorgeous Korean woman in that time (long story).

In the end, though, I missed my parents, sisters and cousins, who increasingly – and alarmingly – felt like strangers to me with each visit I made to Toronto, usually once every two years. Our ongoing lives on opposite ends of the globe created a cultural wedge between us that spread over time like a cracked windshield. I was afraid our personal interests and experiences would grow so far apart that we'd have nothing in common except for our DNA. And I did miss Canada – particularly playing shinny hockey and watching NHL games on TV (I still followed NHL news from Korea) – its more forgiving pace of life and its multicultural diversity, the red and white and the variety of color in between.

"Hello, what can I get for you?" the Korean Air stewardess asked me with a beaming smile and large hyper-attentive eyes.

"Um, do you have any wine?" I said in a gravelly voice. I had just awoken from a nap.

"Yes, would you like red or white, sir?"

"Uh, red, please."

A few minutes later, the stewardess returned with a glass of the red filled to the brim.

"Here is your glass of red wine, sir," she said as she leaned over the two passengers seated next to me and placed it on my tray.

"Thank you," I said.

The wine's oaky aroma and the stewardess' citrus perfume mingled and lingered in the air around me, luring me out of my drowsy stupor.

I sat up straight in my seat. I picked up my glass and looked out the window of the plane. I could see my hair pasted to the back of my head in the reflection. "Great, I have airplane seat hair," I muttered. I tried to fluff it back out with my free hand.

We were flying over the vast expanse of the Pacific Ocean, and it would be another 10 long hours before I arrived in Toronto. After a few sips of the wine, I sank further back into my seat and reflected on my time on that tiny peninsula behind me. When all was said and done, what was originally going to be four years of studying in Korea ballooned into 12 years of studying and working. I shook my head in disbelief.

That was the story of my life.

The ideas that would play out in my head – I called it "theory" – and what would actually transpire in reality were constantly out of sync. The two did not good friends make. Theory said "wake up and smell the roses," while reality said "wake up and smell the cow poop."

Let's recap, I thought: I envisioned studying Oriental philosophy at SNU but wound up completing my B.A. in English. I had imagined I'd be spending endless days pondering life's big questions at the Korean Buddhist monastery, and yet I had a tighter schedule there than when I lived in Seoul. I had envisioned the ideal career path – now five and counting, if you include hockey – within what I was beginning to see were the pristine and palatial confines of my mind. Once I actually left the palace grounds and hit the road, I ran into mudslides, steep hills and potholes.

It wasn't all bad, though. It sometimes worked the other way, too: my father embodied the acidic Old School style of teaching I came to despise as a kid. It was a severe and unnecessary approach, in my mind. Until Old School served as the vehicle through which I felt accepted, at last, as a Pansori student.

I saw the SNU speeches as but cruel and unusual forms of punishment, until Speech extended its warm hands and offered refuge amidst the sometimes cold and demanding environment of journalism. What were once the sources of evil shifted into the sources of good.

I remembered the Korean proverb *Sae-ong-ji-ma*, which I had first heard from my thesis supervisor at Dongguk. (I later discovered the proverb was based on an ancient Chinese Taoist parable and better known in English as "Who Knows What's Good or Bad?") While I "got" its message when I first heard it, it didn't exactly shake me to my core. Tonight, however, it did feel a little like turbulence:

[I'm paraphrasing here.]

There once lived a farmer and his horse. One day, the horse ran away. Word spread quickly in the village, and the other residents consoled the farmer every time they bumped into him in the marketplace.

"I'm so sorry about your horse. To lose your horse is to lose your livelihood."

"Well, who knows if it's a good or bad thing, eh?" the farmer said cheerfully.

The villagers scratched their heads.

One day, the horse that ran away returned. But she returned with several male horses. (She must have been quite the catch!) When the farmer returned to the marketplace the next day, the locals reveled in his good fortune.

"How right you were! Lucky man," each of them would say.

"Well, who knows if that's a good or bad thing, eh?" the farmer would reply in the same cheery voice.

The villagers thought he was a little strange when they heard this.

One day, the farmer's son was riding one of the male horses when he was thrown and broke his leg.

"Oh my Buddha! I heard the news. I hope your son is recovering," the villagers would say to him.

"You know what? I don't know if the accident's a good or bad thing," the farmer would reply.

That was the confirmation the villagers needed. They now knew for certain the farmer was clinically insane.

A month later, officials from the army came knocking on the farmer's door.

"War is imminent," one of them said sternly, "and conscription is now the law of the land. How old is your son?"

"He's 25," the farmer said.

"He qualifies," the official said. "And his health?"

"Well, he's nursing a broken leg, eh?" the farmer said.

The official asked to see the son, who limped his way to the door.

"He's exempt. Good day," the official said.

Who knows what's good or bad, eh?

13
Pins and Needles

Standing on the corner of an intersection in a sleepy neighbourhood of Toronto called North York was the Sheppard Centre. It was a charming little shopping mall with shops one could browse through in under two hours. Tucked away in a far corner of the first floor was a post office. It was the loner of the first floor, at the foot of the darkened concourse leading to Sheppard subway station, where busy patrons descending the stairs to catch the subway only noticed its signage accidentally, in their peripheral vision. I liked to call it The Little Post Office That Could because business was steady and good, despite its location. Ensconced in the right-hand side corner of the post office was a sleek Internet café with a laminate wooden paneled floor called *iClick*.

I sat on a low black leather chair behind *iClick's* cashier counter, only the top half of my head visible to customers when they walked in through the entrance doors. I was practically hidden and invisible, and that's just the way I liked it.

Nunes was the new manager of the post office after taking over for my parents. I volunteered to help out on a casual basis. Life grounded to a snail's pace in my new world. I was the only one working the cash there. There was no rush to meet any deadlines, no after-work gatherings at which to give public speeches and no stress to fuel drinking binges.

I went from living with 10 million to four million people, literally overnight. Gone were the bumps to my shoulder and handprints on my shirt when I rode the Toronto buses or subway. Sidewalk debris freely whipped around along the pavement without constantly being stomped on by pedestrians. The ringing of car horns in my ears had vanished, as had the moments of temporary neon-light blindness. I breathed in clear air rather than smokestacks or car exhaust. The empirical evidence bore that out: when I picked my nose, my boogers were no longer black.

I returned to speaking full-time in the language that came most naturally to me (except to my parents), although I would stutter at times because the Korean word or phrase would bud to the front of the line and come to mind first. This, however, was the last remaining relic from my time spent in Korea, which now felt a million miles away, like some mist-shrouded land I had lived in in a past life. It was as though all my connecting tentacles to that past had been severed at the source once I stepped on Canadian soil, and I then walked straight into an old neighborhood bar where nobody knew my name. But I did feel freer, like I was cut loose from an entangled web.

I also moved back into my old room at my folks' place on top of Crosstown Discount, where I didn't have to agonize about what to cook or where to go out to eat for a change. My mom, who, along with my father, was now retired, looked a little older, her short black hair showing streaks of grey around the edges, her almond-shaped eyes further drooping at the sides and her once pudgy frame more skinny and frail.

My mom cooked up a storm every chance she had. Our house filled with the grilled aroma of Korean-style ribs most evenings. I could tell she was trying to make up for lost time, that is, 12 years' worth of missed opportunities to spoil one of her babies. "You know, I didn't eat this well when you were in Korea," my father once joked.

That was one of the few times I saw any sign of life in my father's eyes. He didn't say much to me after I returned. He didn't have to: "I immigrated all the way to Canada, worked 16-hour days and invested all that money in my son so he could eventually not know what he wanted to do with his life?" – was the thought I imagined those smoldering eyes were holding back.

Or maybe he had just mellowed in his old age? No, that's probably my imagination talking, I thought. Just because my father's shoulders hunched over more while he walked – with slower, heavier steps – didn't mean he'd become more easygoing. Besides, why else would he have taken me aside one morning to tell me about the old Korean proverb *Yong Du Sa Mi*? The four words literally mean "head of a dragon, tail of a snake," a hybrid animal, of sorts, that personifies the person who begins an endeavor with an explosion of inspiration, hope and promise, only to see that inspiration, hope and promise peter out in relatively short order. Such an animal, the proverb cautions, lacks the staying power to succeed.

And he couldn't have been happy that I was mangling the role of Traditional Korean Son. I was 33, single, career-less and back to living at home. I should have had a stable income, a large suburban house and a wife and kids by now. And one of my kids would be a son who could continue the family name. Meanwhile, Nunes and Heejeh were doing well for themselves. Nunes ran the post office, she had her own condo and she was getting serious with Roy, a second-generation Korean-Canadian. Heejeh was the head administrator at the printing shop run by her fiancé, Orion Armstrong, and they had begun shopping around for their forever home.

One day, an elderly yet stocky Asian man carrying a plastic shopping bag walked into the post office. He stopped at the back of the line but, as soon as he glanced over to his right and saw me, he sauntered over my way.

"Do you wok heyuh?" he said, smiling. His English had a familiar Korean accent.

"Yes, I do," I said as I stood up from my chair. It wasn't polite to sit while someone older spoke to you while standing.

"You should be proud," he said. "Dis is good post office. I come heyuh ebury day."

"Oh, good," I said, careful to enunciate clearly and speak slowly lest he didn't understand. I remembered what it felt like when I was in his shoes. "I'm helping my sister. She's the manager here."

"Ohhhh, good. Ha, ha. Dat is you-uh sistuh?" he said, pointing to her behind the post office counter.

"Yes, that's her."

"Ha, ha. You look duh same," he said, his mouth opening up into a circle.

"Well, thank you ... I think," I said.

I was itching to tell him I could speak Korean, but I sensed he wanted to practice his English.

"You know acupunc-chuh? I come from der now."

"Oh. You mean you just came from an acupuncture clinic?"

"Yes, yes. You know Jaseng Dang Clinic? Around heyuh."

"No, I don't."

"Ohhh ..." he said in a hushed tone, as if I should be ashamed of myself for having missed out on something great all these years.

"Berry good acupunc-chuh. Doctuh Lee is Mastuh. I go his school."

My ears perked up.

"Oh, so the doctor at the clinic runs a school, too? Acupuncture school?"

"Yes ... late-uh."

"Later? Oh, not now. When?"

"Soon, maybe end ub dis yeyuh."

End of the year? I thought. That was still several months away. The old gentleman reached into his pocket.

"You call," he said, shoving the clinic's business card into my hand. It must have been obvious to him I was genuinely curious.

The man then shook my hand and slowly walked to the back of the line to wait his turn. I looked down at my wilted right hand. For someone who looked to be in his 60s, the man had one helluva firm handshake.

I sat back down at my desk, gave the desktop computer mouse a good shake and opened up Internet Explorer. I looked up Dr. Lee and the Jaseng Dang Clinic. I discovered Dr. Lee was a Korean acupuncturist and the third-generation torchbearer to a storied family lineage of Oriental Medicine (OM) doctors. When I later called the clinic, Dr. Lee said he wanted to "give back" to the community by training the next generation of acupuncturists, for free. The classes would also be conducted in Korean. No problem, I thought.

My curiosity was piqued. I remembered my interest in Western medicine in my last year of high school. I remembered the exotic yet calming aroma of burning mugwort I breathed in whenever I walked into an OM clinic in Seoul. I recalled the words of a Dongguk classmate who once said there was a "close affinity" between OM and Eastern philosophy, including Buddhism.

A light bulb went off in my head. Greater forces were at work here. OM was a match made in the Buddhist Pure Land – a coalescing of an earlier high school dream and my later studies in Buddhism. My chance meeting with this elderly Korean man was not chance but fate, and he was meant to introduce me to Dr. Lee. As an added bonus, the training I'd receive from him wouldn't cost me a dime.

I must keep the faith, I told myself. I repeated my mantra under my breath: even if this doesn't work out, I will come out the better for it, in some useful way. *Believe, Glen.*

Over the next several days, inspiration swelled within me and my powers of imagination took over:

Basking in a vast ocean of ancient Eastern knowledge and wisdom, I leisurely stroll into my clinic office one early morning in my long flowing navy blue Korean robe.

As I open the door to my OM clinic in Toronto, I am welcomed by the exotic and enchanting scent of burnt mugwort lingering in the air, olfactory vestiges of moxibustion therapy from the previous day.

A small gilt statue of the Buddha in meditative repose watches over me on the shelf above my head as I sit cross-legged on the bamboo mat sprawled across my office floor. My ears are tickled by the gurgling sound of boiling water in the electric kettle next to me. To my left lies a low-floor antique wooden tea table in the natural shape of a tree trunk, on top of which sits a small traditional Korean ceramic tea cup, patiently waiting to be filled.

I gently tug on my long and thick black beard as I sip on a cup of steaming green tea. I am locked in deep contemplations about the classical Eastern interpretations on the origins of disease.

My first client of the day arrives promptly at 9 a.m. She complains about chronic pain in her shoulders. After taking her pulse, I deftly and effortlessly insert three acupuncture needles in three different locations around her shoulder blades and abdomen area.

Before long, her pain has subsided, and she flashes a brilliant smile at the wonders of acupuncture therapy. I prescribe a concoction of dried herbal powder to be taken with water thrice a day and send her on her way.

"So you have an M.A. in Buddhism from Korea, is that correct?" Prof. Sugunasiri said as he put away his files into his briefcase, ready to call it a day.

"Yes," I said.

"So what do you see yourself doing in the future?" he said, stopping momentarily.

I hesitated. We had just concluded our weekly Friday afternoon meeting in Prof. Sugunasiri's office, where I debriefed him on the state of administrative affairs at the Nalanda College of Buddhist Studies, a small and recently started private college in Toronto that awarded a certificate in Buddhist Studies. Prof. Sugunasiri, an elderly white-haired gentleman of Sri Lankan descent, founded the college and was currently serving as its president. I was recently hired as a part-time registrar, three days per week, four hours each day.

I got the position accidentally. I had decided to leave *iClick* and look for gainful, albeit temporary, work before the start of the OM program. The money I had saved from my days as a journalist wouldn't sustain me long-term. I sent out feelers to a number of postsecondary institutions inquiring about Korean-language teaching positions – I had never taught a course before, and I wanted to try something different. I was more qualified to teach Korean (at least, spoken Korean) than Buddhism, since I only had an M.A. in the latter and hadn't touched the subject academically for the last three years. (I was pretty sure you needed a Ph.D. to teach.) The Korean language, on the other hand, was something I had spent the last 12 years sculpting and refining. Nalanda didn't offer a Korean-language course, not yet anyway, but it did have an opening for registrar.

"If you want to teach at the university level, you do know you'll need a doctorate," he continued.

I didn't want to tell him about my dreams of acupuncture needles and herbal concoctions just yet, just in case that didn't pan out either. I was more mindful of my track record these days.

"Yes, I do know that. I haven't given the Ph.D. much thought, to be honest. It's just that ... it would be quite a ... commitment."

"Oh, indeed, it would. You have to be wholly committed, without question, or you won't be able to finish."

Prof. Sugunasiri had completed his doctorate almost three decades ago, in 1978.

"Yes, that's what I thought," I said.

We left it at that, and I wished him a good day. I returned to my office, which was literally five steps next door to his, to finish up the Nalanda graduation certificate template on MS Word. I was the only regular employee of Nalanda, to go along with a very part-time accountant and a volunteer Board of Directors whom I would see a couple of times per semester. It didn't take too many warm bodies to cover the work, since a semester averaged between five and 10 registered students and our faculty consisted of six part-time professors.

I did admire Prof. Sugunasiri. He came to every meeting nattily clad in a fresh-pressed suit and tie with briefcase in hand, looking like he was ready to talk business and meant business. It was probably that attitude that made him a celebrity figure of sorts in the Buddhist community in Toronto, launching one initiative after another to raise Buddhism's public profile, not the least of which was this college. He was also currently moonlighting as an adjunct professor at the vaunted University of Toronto, one of the universities at which I dreamt about teaching once upon a time. And it was the Ph.D. that had opened that door for him.

Three months after I got the Nalanda job, I heard back from the University of Toronto's School of Continuing Studies, one of the other places I had earlier reached out to. After submitting my resumé and other documents – including a certificate issued by a third party that verified the Canadian equivalency of SNU's and Dongguk's academic credentials – and participating in a phone and in-person interview, I was offered the recently vacated *Speak Korean* instructor position. I couldn't have timed my application any better. The position would begin in the coming fall, one evening per week, two hours each time, which didn't conflict with my work at Nalanda.

On a windswept Monday evening in October, I arrived for my first Korean class at OISE, a hulking 12-storey concrete building on the University of Toronto's campus. Unlike SNU or Dongguk, I couldn't trace where the U of T campus started and ended. Its edifices blended in with the rest of the salad bowl of sleek modernist commercial buildings and a scattering of Victorian and Gothic-style heritage homes in Toronto's downtown core.

I got off the elevator on the third floor and walked onto the thin yet compact carpet, which was easy on the knees even with my leather-heeled dress shoes on. I stepped into Room 3311. The stench of old tomes and contemplative sweat lingered in the air. I looked around. The classroom set-up threw me off because the room and tables seemed to stretch sideways rather than up-down like most classrooms I knew.

I looked up at the clock on the wall at the front of the room. It was 6:35 p.m. None of the eight students registered for the course had yet arrived. I walked over to the chalkboard to check for chalks and an eraser and then over to the thick wooden lectern, on top of which I rested my knapsack.

I took out my textbook and lesson-plan sheet and reviewed it one last time for several minutes. Five minutes later the students began trickling in. By 7 p.m., everyone had arrived. I performed a quick surreptitious self-scan of my navy blue V-neck sweater, which I deliberately wore with the shirt collar out as a fashion statement, and my new white khakis I had bought at the Gap. Good, no lint and no open fly.

"Hi, everyone," I finally said, clasping my hands.

"I'm your instructor for this class, Glen Choi. I'm glad to meet all of you, and I look forward to a great semester together."

This was my go-to opening-line template, the pattern for which I had perfected from my days in Korea. It felt somewhat awkward, however, saying this both in English and to a fully non-Korean audience for the first time.

"… And by the end of the semester, my goal is to make sure you all speak like native Koreans."

The class laughed. Making people laugh never got old. I was ready to dive into the first lesson when I thought of something on the spot.

"So before we begin," I said, "I just wanted to know your names and what your motivations are for learning Korean. Let's go around the room, one by one, starting with you on my right."

"Oh, okay. Hi, everyone. My name is Jack. I'm taking this class because my wife is Korean, and I just thought it'd be good to learn more about her native language."

"Hi, my name's Greg, and I'm learning because my wife is Korean, and I'd like to speak it a bit so I can communicate with my in-laws."

"Hi, my name's Sarah. My boyfriend's Korean and, like the others, I want to learn more because of that."

"Hi, my name's Jean. My boyfriend is also Korean," she said to a round of giggles, "and like Sarah and the others, I too want to learn Korean so we don't always have to communicate in a language he's not entirely comfortable with."

Right then I playfully raised both my hands in objection.

"Maybe a better question to have started with," I said, "is 'how many of you are here for reasons other than romantic relationships?'"

Another round of laughter.

By the end of the introductions, all but one of the eight students cited their partners as their motivating factor to learn.

"Okay, well thank you all for sharing," I said, readying to get a little more personal myself. "As for me, my story's not quite as romantic as yours … Well, it is but in a different way. I romanticized a lot about my career, that's for sure."

I gave the group the drastically condensed version of my story.

"That's crazy," Greg said, "that you went back and did all that."

"Yeah, well," I said, breaking into a smile, "I'm a crazy guy. No, seriously, I guess you could say I was crazy about finding my one passion in life … and still searching, by the way."

The students and I bantered for a few more minutes.

"Great. So let's get started," I said as my voice transitioned into a more serious tone.

"I'm going to talk a little bit about Korean culture before we move on to the exercises in our textbook. Why? Well, they say you can't learn a language without understanding the culture first. Do you agree with that statement?"

I could hear murmurs of "yes," "yep" and "uhuh."

"Well, why do you think that is?"

There was a brief pause before John, an older man and clearly the Elder of the bunch, raised his hand.

"Yes," I said, pointing to him.

This was surreal. Only yesterday, it seemed, was I the subordinate student who raised his hand and hoped the teacher would pick; now here I was today, a teacher who wielded all the power to dictate and delegate.

"I think," John said, choosing his words carefully, "a lot of expressions are culture-specific. Like your frame of reference …"

"Yeah," Jean said, "and how you say things, like your intonation."

"Yes, that's very good," I said in as baritone a voice as I could muster so as to leave no doubt among the students that I was an absolute authority on the topic.

"Let me give you an example," I said. I was excited to dig into my vaunted memory bank of experiences in Korea.

"In English, when we tell others about the school we attend or the home we live in, how do we refer to the school or the home?"

Silence.

"Sorry, what do you mean exactly … ?" Sarah said.

"Sorry," I said. "I'm not expressing myself clearly here. What I mean is, we say 'my school,' as in 'that's my school' in English. Or 'my house,' 'that's my house.' So we use the possessive pronoun 'my,' is what I'm trying to say here."

More murmurs of agreement, except for one.

"Well, not necessarily," John said. "We'll say 'our house' sometimes, depending on the situation …"

"That's right," I said, pausing for a moment to gather my thoughts. "So if you're with your family and, say, you're pointing out your house to some stranger, yeah, in English we'll say 'that's our house.'"

"Right," John said.

"But if you're alone," I said, "and pointing out your house to some stranger, we'll then say 'that's my house, over there.'"

"But in Korean, we say 'our school,' 'our home,' regardless of the situation."

"Why is that?" Jean interrupted. "It sounds strange to use 'our' when you're not with anybody … like your family."

"Good question. Well, Korean culture emphasizes the group, the collective, more than we do here in Canada, where we're more about the individual. That's not to say we're more selfish here or anything like that. It's just a different culture."

"Okay …" said Jean, waiting to hear more.

"So even when Koreans are alone and pointing out their home, or school, to some stranger, they're always thinking in the collective. Their identity is more group-based. The groups they're a part of, like family or workplace, are like extensions of the self."

I didn't want to sound too technical. But the class seemed to be getting it.

"So if you go to Korea," I continued, "and say 'my school' or 'my family' in Korean, the natives might think 'what, so you own the family!?'"

More chuckles and laughter.

When I returned home that night, the adrenaline I felt from teaching had yet to subside. I had so much to say and stories to share, and it felt therapeutic to get this off my chest. I was already looking forward to next week. For a moment, the idea of going back to school to do a Ph.D. flashed across my mind, if only so I could teach at the postsecondary level, for a living.

"Aghh!" I screamed in my head as I slowly lowered an acupuncture needle into an area between my thumb and forefinger.

Although the needle had yet to puncture my skin, I winced in anticipation of the prickly pain, as well as the gore of seeing blood squirt left, right and center. And then I might faint, like the one time a doctor drew blood from a vein in my arm and, when I came to, I had an apple growing out of my head. The internalized scream was my way of allaying my fears.

"Here, stick it in my hand," the elderly man I had met at the post office said to me. "There's nothing to be afraid of."

The man had switched to speaking in Korean to me after he realized I could speak the language. We were sitting next to each other in a classroom of about 20 mostly middle-aged Korean immigrant men and women, during an acupuncture practicum. Dr. Lee had rented a classroom at a nearby high school.

"Umm, okay," I responded in Korean.

I slowly pushed the needle down.

"No. Push harder," he said.

"That's as far as it'll go," I said. The conversation sounded a little raunchy.

"No, it goes deeper. See?"

He twisted and prodded the top end of the needle to sink it deeper into the soft webby area of his hand, until only the tip remained visible.

"But doesn't it hurt?" I said, crinkling my nose.

"No, of course not," he replied with a sadistic grin. "It feels good."

I learned that the elderly man was a former Korean Marine, which explained his high threshold for physical pain. And the good he felt was likely somewhere around his intestine, at least according to OM theory: stimulating that particular pressure point along the hand promotes the overall flow of chi, the basic life force that circulates throughout the body along energy channels called "meridians." It's especially effective against indigestion, which is stagnant chi in the stomach.

The body and its nearly 400 acupuncture points were interwoven together by thread upon thread of energy channels. The acupuncture dummy we were shown during the practicum looked like he had the convoluted Seoul subway map tattooed over the entirety of his body; the meridians were the subway lines that connected the hundreds of subway stations that were the pressure points. If I had an upset stomach growing up, my mom would give me two tablespoons of Pepto Bismol, which worked like a charm. I assumed it was effective because it actually targeted the stomach, the intrinsic source of the problem. Such tunnel vision, retorted OM, the remedy for which lay in the extrinsic ties that bind.

Koreans, I curiously noted, seemed to have this quasi-fetish with context and connections: my SNU classmates and *Korea Herald* colleagues and I were roped together and made "one" by way of the countless social gatherings; a person's identity was inextricably tied to the specific social situation in Master Daehaeng's teachings; and the hundreds of acupuncture points dotting the human body were threaded together by way of the meridian lines. It was as though the word "separation" was a negligible noun in the Korean lexicon, the antagonist in the story about the interconnectedness of all things, the shady yin to the illuminating yang of oneness. What we might see as individual parts, Koreans admonished, were not oxbow lakes but curves and swerves along the road – same basic asphalt substance, different shapes, never severed.

In any event, that wasn't important right now. What was important was this: I had recently completed a chunk of the theoretical portion of the OM program and, overall, it wasn't looking good for me. From afar, the acupuncture needle was a panacea. Contained within this shiny, sleek, innocuous and beautiful silver ornament was the Oriental secret to curing all that ailed the patient. When it finally came time to actually hold one up close and stick it deep inside my hand, it became a thick, ugly, sterile, menacing and blood-gushing utensil.

This was an immediate red flag for me. If I had deep, unresolved personal issues about puncturing my own skin with any kind of instrument, how would I ever be able to perform this on a future patient? Acupuncture was a foundational treatment modality in the repertoire of OM doctors, and there would be no way around it. I was also reluctant to put in the time and money to see a psychologist about my issue.

This harrowing experience came fresh off the heels of the discovery that, based on the introductory OM theory course, my Buddhist background wouldn't help me in any substantial or practical way. I saw philosophical compatibility between the two – again, that crowning of the idea that all things are interdependent – but it began and ended with that. Instead, I was now leafing through books on Taoism after one of my OM classmates told me that this indigenous Chinese philosophy was far more relevant.

I was also learning a whole new language with OM – the language of meridians, acupressure points in Sino-Korean and Romanized Chinese, and medical-philosophical principles like the Five Elements Theory. I was required to memorize the location of hundreds of acupressure points, the complex interplay between the major bodily organs and hundreds more classical Chinese characters than the few hundred I retained after I left the Buddhist monastery.

Alas, my once youthful vigor that propelled me through the initial rough patches of a new career started to wear thin and showed signs of cracking. No longer did I have the energy to climb even the first few steps. I felt like a grizzled boxer whose chin was deteriorating after a long and dubious career. I had recently turned 34, and OM represented my sixth attempt at finding the perfect career match. I was getting too old for this.

The thought that I was doomed to a life of dissatisfaction – that I could never be satisfied no matter what line of work I pursued – crept into my head. I began to question whether my long-harbored belief in the "greater reason" – that my past experiences would all coalesce one day in service of a single and almost divine end goal – was, in fact, a lie I told myself. Was I spinning the wheels of delusional positivity so I could continue to live in blissful denial? If this was true, that would mean the trust I had put into the invisible hand of destiny, the basic building blocks of my belief about the way the world worked, was founded on quicksand.

Was my time in Korea, then, simply one long drawn-out lesson in focus and perseverance, which I failed to heed? Was the answer simply to stay the course in one thing, whether I liked it or not? So what if I had diverse academic and work experiences. This all cowered in the disgruntled face of that hybrid Korean beast *Yong Du Sa Mi*. In Canada, I saw the smug face of the Jack of All Trades, Master of None, saying "tsk, tsk, tsk."

To add insult to injury, I had to let go of the one activity that would bring a smile to my face, teaching Korean. After my first semester of teaching, I learned that the weekday evening OM classes clashed with my Korean classes (I was able to continue to work at Nalanda, though). I had no choice. Oriental medicine was going to be my career, and my teaching gig would have to be the sacrificial lamb to appease the grander picture. I didn't give it a second thought at the time.

In the summer break after my first semester of OM school, Dr. Lee announced he'd be using the next semester to revamp the school's curriculum, so there would be no classes in the coming fall. I decided to make use of the time off by finding a second part-time job, something to have in addition to Nalanda. So I applied to the Whole Foods Market store in downtown Toronto, near the college in fact, and was hired as a Maintenance team member soon after.

I didn't care what kind of work I did there, as long as I had the opportunity to do three things. First, to learn about the latest in natural and alternative health products on the market. I thought I could do this by observing, listening or talking to my more knowledgeable co-workers, and that having this kind of knowledge could benefit my potential future practice as an OM doctor.

Second, get lots of physical activity. I was more than ready to ditch the office chair and desktop computer in favor of walking, bending, crouching and lifting all day. I wanted to get my blood pumping and my endorphins flowing for a change.

Third, make more money, even if it was minimum wage and part-time.

I started with four-hour shifts three times a week at Whole Foods. Wearing a black apron and cap, essentially the employee uniform, I attacked the store floors as though I'd just been released into society after serving time. The store every day filled with the aroma of herbs and spices, freshly baked pastries and pizza, and freshly brewed organic coffee. I hunted the aisles for shopping cart skid marks and the bulk food section for raisin roadkill, mopped the former and scraped and swept the latter into the dust pan, soaped down the elevator walls, and spick-and-spanned the public washrooms. When customers came to me with a question about our selection of gluten-free or hypoallergenic beauty products, I'd chase down a co-worker in the grocery or beauty department, after which I'd hang around so I could learn myself. If customers asked where the washrooms were, I'd oftentimes escort them all the way to the door.

I also enjoyed the camaraderie among the staff. I came to work looking forward to teasing Liz, who had just started her undergraduate degree, from Coffee; learning a new Spanish word from the other Maintenance guy, a fiftysomething man who was of Ecuadorian descent; and bantering with Don from Prepared Foods. With a well-groomed salt-and-pepper beard and thick black-rimmed glasses, Don looked like he was in the wrong profession. He looked more like a writer – a writer on *Seinfeld*, that is. He could take a seemingly trivial matter and magnify its philosophical significance twentyfold:

> **Don**: I don't think it's proper to say "I'm sorry" to strangers when, say, you bump into them on the street. It's like you're degrading yourself in a way when you say this. Because you are saying sorry for your existence. Why are you sorry? It's more proper to say "excuse me" or "pardon me." It's more assertive and self-affirming.
> **Me**: I see what you're saying. But maybe you're overanalyzing this. "I'm sorry" is just habit, a knee-jerk response. They're not necessarily saying this because they lack self-esteem. That's a big leap.
> **Don**: I disagree. It's at the subconscious level that this self-degradation occurs …
> **Whole Foods Manager** (who happened to walk by at that moment): Are you guys on break? If not, please get back to work.

Four months flew by at Whole Foods before it happened again. My energy began to wane. I started to feel pain in my muscles and joints after I finished cleaning or mopping something. Instead of escorting customers to the washroom door, I started to point in its general direction. Rather than clocking into work several minutes early, I dared clock in a few minutes late from time to time. Instead of a new day at work, each day became like the same old day. Even the smell of coffee, pastry and herbs began to reek of the foreboding of yet another mind-numbing work shift.

One afternoon, I returned to the Whole Foods employee backroom after mopping down the produce section. I rinsed the mop in the maintenance closet sink and was in the middle of dumping a bucket full of dark murky water when an announcement came over the loud speaker: "Maintenance to Customer Service, Maintenance to Customer Service, thank you."

I quickly finished up what I was doing, poured clean water into the bucket and headed right back on the floor. With one hand on the mop handle, I pushed the squeaky wheels of the yellow bucket with my other hand and made my way to Customer Service. When I arrived at the scene of the crime, I saw a small pool of what looked like clam chowder soup on the floor. A customer must have accidentally dropped the container on his way out, I thought. This was not uncommon. I noticed a leashed dog by the Customer Service booth, staring out into the sea of customers, bopping his head trying to catch sight of his owner.

As I lifted the mop onto the mop wringer, my Customer Service co-worker rushed over with a wry smile.

"Ugh, the dog just threw up. I know, disgusting. I feel bad asking you, but can you please clean that up? Thanks, Glen!" she said in a speedy and cheery voice.

"No problem," I said with my best poker face.

When I returned to the backroom to throw out the contents of the bucket, I leaned on my mop stick and heaved a deep sigh. Am I really learning a lot about health products by working here? I thought to myself. Why don't I just research about them?

My original plans were falling apart. The disillusionments with and delay in the OM program, and now I was second-guessing my decision to work at Whole Foods.

I clocked out for my 15-minute break. I took off my apron and cap in the back-room, threw on my winter coat and strolled out onto the store floor, my hands tucked inside my jean pockets. I felt like walking outside in the snow to clear my head. I got on the escalator.

As I made my ascent, I thought about a Korean proverb my father mentioned that was encouraging, for a change. It meshed well with my mantra. *Dae Gi Man Sung*. A truly great person achieves success late in life. The great ones are late bloom-ers, is what I heard. That's because you had to be ripe before you were ready, ready to tackle greater projects and do great things in life. The ripening process required years and years … of different life experiences … that, however, were held together by a common thread. A generally forward motion, not too backward or lateral. You needed to be consistent with one thing and bolster it with different things along the way. Because both the one and the many experiences would come to mix, mingle and marinate one day, and the finished product would be a dynamic you. Ideally, theoretically, I was formulating.

I thought about the Ph.D. once again. Maybe I was now ripe and ready to do it. It had been 11 years since I entered SNU. About half of those years I spent in school; the other half I invested in life experiences.

Just before I punched back in for work, I made up my mind. It was time to move on. Move on from Whole Foods and from Oriental medicine. The whole nine yards. It was time to come full circle, to take the Ph.D. plunge. I no longer cared for the ivy tower, the cushy black leather chair, smoking on pipes, and the navy blue cardigan sweater. I just wanted to get in, graduate and get a teaching job.

I had to first come up with a plan, though. I remembered an academic confer-ence that Nalanda hosted about a year ago, which I attended as the college registrar. Among the presenters was a sociology of religion professor from a university four hours up the road, the University of Ottawa, who talked about Buddhism in Can-ada, including the religiosities of the children of Asian Buddhist immigrants. I didn't even know this could be a topic for academic research. He had my attention because he was basically giving a talk about my peeps, us double-minority Korean Buddhist underdogs, the David to the Christian Goliath. Unfortunately, I forgot the professor's name. I looked him up online and found him: Peter Beyer. I was about to send him an e-mail about my idea to do research on the younger generation of Korean Bud-dhists in Canada. If he liked it, I'd ask him to be my thesis advisor.

I felt good about my decision. I was finally going to take the path of least resistance. A Ph.D. after the M.A., and in a field related to Buddhism. I wouldn't have to reinvent myself like I did with most of my other past pursuits. At least I'd be starting halfway up the cliff if I did the doctorate, instead of at the bottom. Then, once I was done, I'd get to teach in a university for a living.

I wasn't the only one who felt good about the decision.

"Oh, really?" my father said after I walked in on him sitting in my room one late afternoon. As usual, he was sitting on the hazel-nut velvet sofa that Nunes had donated to my parents. His feet were propped up on a chair, and he was watching an English premier soccer match on cable TV, in his wine-colored pajamas. My mom was hogging the main TV in the living room, watching a Korean soap opera.

He hauled himself up on his seat and put his feet to the floor. I could make out the glimmer of a spark in his eyes. "A Ph.D. is very good. Not anyone can do it. Good, good."

I told him about the University of Ottawa and Peter Beyer.

"And you wouldn't be that far from home. How convenient," he said.

"And if I qualify, I could receive a scholarship," I said, getting excited because my father was finally showing some life. "So no tuition."

"That's very good. Anyway, don't worry about money. I'll do my best to support you, if you need it. But this is the last time," he said breaking into a half-smile. "You know I'm old now, I'm 68, you should be supporting your mom and me right now."

"Yes, thank you for all your support," I said. *Ugh*. I sounded again like a polished politician. I did surprise myself, though. This was probably the first time I ever thanked him, explicitly, for anything. And it felt very awkward, emasculating almost, as if expressing any kind of sentimentality in front of him was a sign of beta weakness.

"You know," he said in a voice tinged with nostalgia, "when I was your age, that was when I immigrated to Canada. I had to financially provide for our family, my brothers and sister when they first came to Canada, my parents."

He paused, then chuckled. "Did you know, when I first came here in 1971, I had $5 in my pocket? Five dollars. I lost a chunk of it on the first day after landing at Pearson airport. I didn't know how to use the public phones."

"Yes, I think you told me that before."

"Your mom and I," he continued, "we had to give up our high school teaching jobs in Seoul to make money in Canada. I started out at the CCM factory, then convenience store, post office … Anyway, what I'm saying is, I wanted to study more, but there was no time. Your generation, the second-generation Koreans, you're very lucky you can."

PART III
A World of Dots

14
A Fresh Start

It was a clear and sunny April day. As I walked toward Ottawa U's campus, I could see sweeping swaths of the blue sky from most spots. Unlike Toronto, lines of low-rises dominated Ottawa's downtown landscape. The streets were quiet, interrupted only by the swishing of cars driving by. I noticed a lot of business and traffic signs written in French and heard French being spoken here and there among passersby. Canada's official policy of English-French bilingualism was no longer something I heard about on TV or read about in the newspaper; I was now living it. I'd better pick up my French, I thought. Although I had moved just up the road, it felt strange, like I was in a different country and culture.

A stone's throw south of the downtown core was the campus, neatly encased within a rectangular plot of land. I tried to make sense of the heavily creased campus map in my right hand as I navigated my way west to the Arts building.

I arrived. I went up to the second floor and down a dimly lit corridor. Not a single student in sight. It was Monday, but it felt like Sunday. Probably because this was the last day of April and most students had gone home for the summer break.

I walked along looking at the name tags and room numbers on the wall. Found it: Dr. Peter Beyer.

I knocked on Peter's door, which was slightly ajar.

"Come in," said a voice from inside.

"Hi, Professor Beyer," I said as I opened the door, craned my neck forward and bowed my head. Old habits, as they say, die hard.

Before me sat a slim bespectacled man punching away at his keyboard, his shoulders slightly hunched. His bald scalp on top shone under the fluorescent lights, and the patches of hair on the side and back of his head were graying.

Peter stopped what he was doing and turned to face me.

"You must be Glen!"

Before I could say yes, he said, "Do you know how rare you are!?"

I paused. "Uhh …"

"There are only 260 of you in Canada!" he said. *Right.* I knew what he was talking about because I had read his recent article; he was referring to the stats from the most recent Canadian census. "Where are all of the second-generation Korean Buddhists in Canada? That, I guess, is why you're here."

"Yes, that's right," I said. I was still trying to get my bearings. I sat down on the seat facing his desk.

Peter pulled up his chair to face me. "So your background training is very unusual, given your B.A. specialization and the very focused M.A. you did."

"Yes."

"Speaking of your thesis, it was well-written."

"Thank you," I said, a little surprised.

"The admissions committee wasn't sure about taking you on as a doctoral student, but I said 'have you read his thesis? It's on par with our students.'"

His words echoed in the air. If I had written that in Korean, I might not be sitting here today, I thought.

"So, as you know, you'll have to do some make-up courses for me in the specific discipline of religious studies."

"Yes, I got that e-mail."

For the next several minutes, Peter and I discussed the make-up of these make-up courses.

"Okay, we'll be in touch, then," he said.

"Yes," I said, "I will keep you posted on the readings."

I was feeling good about the whole Ph.D. thing as I exited the Arts building. My advisor seemed cool, the meeting was short and sweet, and my make-up courses were taking shape. And writing my M.A. thesis in English came in handy. That good old "greater reason." An old friend it once was, a foe it had become, an olive branch it was now – maybe, just maybe – extending.

15
Ph.D. = Permanent Head Damage

"FUCK MY SHOELACES," I MUTTERED AFTER stealing a glance at the one lace that had come undone. I closed the door behind me and stepped out onto the deck of the small rustic cabin I was renting in the woods.

If I trip and crack my head open, I wouldn't give a shit, I thought.

I got into my old silver Honda Civic 2000, which I had recently bought used, and drove up the dirt road of my driveway, past my landlord's house on the left and onto the regional highway, where I then sped away toward the university campus.

I was in the fourth year of the Ph.D. program and thick in the throes of writing the dissertation. I had recently moved to the country from the city to be closer to nature and, hopefully, be inspired to read and write a lot more. That was the one thing I loved about Ottawa – you could drive 20 to 30 minutes from downtown before you hit unpaved gravel roads, charming villages, century-old farms with pasturing cattle and horses, magnificent sugar maple trees, luscious rows of ferns, the cacophony of small birds and Canadian geese, and lakes that stretched endlessly toward the horizon.

I stopped by the nearest Tim Hortons on the way for my obligatory morning cup of coffee. I recognized the cashier lady and she me.

"Hi, welcome to Tim Hortons. May I take your order?" she said.

"Do I really have to say?" I said with my eyes half-open thanks to another late night of reading and writing.

She smiled. "Small regular, right?"

"Yes."

I parked my car in my usual spot, a 3-hour free parking zone on a residential street five blocks from the campus. I got out of the car and reached into my pants

133

pocket to look at the time on my iPhone. I should move the car at about 2:30 p.m. to another spot, I told myself.

I walked into Morisset, the university library, with my coffee in hand and a black tote bag full of books slung over my shoulder. I had taken several sips of coffee by this time, so I felt slightly more awake now.

I stepped out of the elevator and onto the sixth floor.

"Hi, Kyuhoon," I said as I walked up to his computer cubicle.

Kyuhoon was a younger colleague in the Religious Studies department. He was a tall and lanky native Korean student doing his Ph.D. abroad.

"Hi, Glen. How are you?" he said in his trademark baritone voice. He spoke with a slight accent to his English.

"Not bad," I said, barely managing a smile. I was lying. "How are you?"

"Oh, you know, tired," he said with a wave of his hand. "But, as you know, we have no choice. We need to graduate sometime."

"Yeah, I hear ya."

I put my bag down on the vacant cubicle next to his. I noticed the crumbs from the muffin I ate last night were still lying there on the desk, something I never would have allowed in my Whole Food days. I nodded my head in the direction of the elevator and Kyuhoon immediately understood: "Wanna go for a coffee to commiserate for a bit?"

"How's your thesis coming along?" I asked him once we sat down in the student lounge on the second floor, coffee cups in hand. This was probably the hundredth time I had asked him that question.

"I'm still refining a couple of chapters," he said. "And how about you? How is the analysis of the Korean Buddhists you interviewed going?"

This was also probably the hundredth time he asked me this question. There really wasn't much else to talk about between us, besides the minus-30 degrees Celsius Ottawa winter weather that we'd have to brave, yet again, in a few months' time.

"It's okay, I guess. The thing is," I said, turning more serious for a moment, "a lot of the young Korean Buddhists don't even go to temple. Some are even Christian, and they practice Buddhism on their own, without affiliation. So how do I fit them into the whole theme of, ya know, what the experts are saying, about how immigrants use the church, the religious institution, as a way to adapt to the New World?"

"But that's great," he said. "Maybe you can find some new pattern. And your topic is great. There's very little information about second-generation Korean Buddhists out there."

"Yeah, true, but it's hard ..."

The real drudgery and monotony would begin once I returned to my cubicle. After turning on the computer, I would stick in my USB flash drive, rest my chin on both hands and let out a deep, heaving sigh knowing that – yet again – it was just me, my books and the computer screen for the next six to seven hours. I would then blankly stare at the sea of data files that appeared before me – sometimes for up to an hour if I allowed my mind to wander – before deciding which to open, read and hopefully cite that day.

The more I read, the more bibliographical links I'd find to books and journal articles related to Canadian immigration, younger generation Koreans in Canada and the U.S., religion and immigration in the West, Korean religions in North America, and North American Buddhism. I was reading books in order to decide which books to read. And the more reading material I found, the more elusive the finish date for my thesis seemed. But I didn't see any escape from this abyss of information; the more experts in the field I could quote and reference, the more comprehensive and authoritative my thesis would be. I had to take a long detour sideways before I could inch forward.

Most days, I'd pray for the inspiration to write one page. I would agonize over whether the paragraph I had just written made sense. If it did, on to the next, and the one after that, and I would feel good about myself, until I realized I still had 200 pages of nuanced analyses left to wring out of my brain.

My way of numbing this pain was to surf the Web, for sometimes four to five hours straight. I always started out with good intentions, however. I told myself I deserved a brief break from the writing. So I checked my e-mail and read the NHL news online. I would then spot a link to a random news story that intrigued me, after which I would find a link to yet another compelling and random story that I had to click and read. Five hours later, I would be deeply immersed in the online world of UFO conspiracy theories and abduction cases, with more than 10 open tabs at the top of my screen that served as a trail of how I ended up on a webpage that had no bearing on my dissertation.

I would visit the library almost every weekday and go to the same floor and sit on the same seat. I'd see the usual suspects on the fourth floor, other graduate students, I assumed. I saw them so often that I could eventually predict the timing of their bowel movements in the evenings.

Every day was like Groundhog Day. I loved the movie when I first watched it back in my Dongguk days, and not only because I saw Buddhist themes in it. I remembered I rubbed my hands with glee when Phil (played by Bill Murray) and his grand sense of entitlement came tumbling down from a pompous perch. Karma's a bitch, however, and I was now living Phil's life. I had become the numb Phil living the same day over and over again.

What got me through these days was knowing a little piece of heaven awaited me at my door when I came home each night: my Tortoise Shell Persian cat named Kitty (I know, how original). I'd open the door, hear a sharp "meow," look down at her long and silky soft white coat, beach-ball round eyes, pudgy nose and her lower bucktooth that jutted out from her mouth when she closed it, as she luxuriated in a stretch on the floor, and only the present moment existed in that moment. When I knelt down to stroke her from head to tail, I forgot about my world outside of our little cabin. I was grateful to Nunes, who had given me Kitty back in my first year lest I'd get lonely living alone in Ottawa. (I'm sure she also thought "get a girlfriend, already.")

16
Ebb and Flow

ANOTHER LAZY SUNDAY AFTERNOON. EARTH was taking its galactic Sabbath from spinning and grinding along its orbit all week, and the silence in my cabin was deafening.

I sat at the long wooden dining table-cum-personal desk at home, in the sun-splashed dining room. I was alone in my pair of white threadbare long johns that frayed around the ankles. My elbows rested on the table and my chin on my fists, and a three quarters-blank MS Word document stared back at me. I decided to take a long hard look at my reflection on the laptop screen.

It was time to call a spade a spade – I was a loser.

I was fast approaching 40 years of age and pocketing an average of just over $1,000 a month doing Teaching/Research Assistantships since I started. I was lucky my scholarship had covered my tuition, but it had a time limit of four years, which was now coming to an end. I yearned for the days I made a solid and steady salary, even if the work at the time did feel like a job. I was investing all of my time and spending every ounce of my energy on writing something clogged with technical jargon. It was a topic so narrow in focus that probably only 10 people in total would read it. In my lifetime. Writing the dissertation seemed like such an elitist endeavor. And I wasn't elitist; I was an impostor. If I had pursued medicine and spent this kind of time and energy, I would have discovered a cure for cancer by now and made a *real* difference.

I was also still single. During dates, I couldn't shake the feeling I was lying to myself and the woman sitting next to or across from me. My convictions and confidence sprung from the belly of identity. Yet I was a fake doctoral student. I acted like a cool and casual intellectual while this glob of insecurity and unhappiness rotted away underneath. It was such an effort to genuinely engage people, even more so a wonderful date I wanted to impress so much.

I estimated that my teaching career wouldn't begin for a good five to 10 years down the road at the rate my dissertation-writing was going. If I was lucky, I would be starting my career at close to 50 years of age, when most people were beginning to contemplate retirement. The ends didn't seem to justify the means. I resented and regretted ever doing the Ph.D.

The added realization that the doctorate represented my seventh stab at a career match poured salt on what was now a profusely bleeding wound. *Seventh.* I mean, who does that? I thought to myself. Everyone around me seemed to know what they wanted to do with their lives, and they were doing it or were well on their way; why couldn't I? I had been experimenting with different careers like some mad scientist all this time, with the emphasis on "mad."

For someone perfecting a career-focused approach to life, this was not how it was supposed to be. I was supposed to have found a career I loved and become the expert in my field by my 30s at the latest. Except for the brief time I considered becoming a Buddhist monk, I imagined I would have settled down by my mid 30s with a lovely wife and kids and lakefront home somewhere with a wraparound cedar deck, sipping on a glass of Zinfandel rose wine while watching the sunset.

I was amazed at how all my dreams meant absolutely nothing.

And that was the last straw.

I was out of gas. Done, kaput, nothing. My engine had petered out and come to a dead stall.

No longer did I have the willpower to pick myself back up and imagine the positive flipside. That mantra had grown tiresome and more difficult to believe by the year, then by the month, more recently by the day, and it had just skidded face-first into a pole. I didn't even have energy to continue my bitching and moaning about all that was currently wrong with my life. I stared down the cold hard truth this time.

> *Universe, you know what?*
> *You win.*
> *It's okay; I don't have to finish the Ph.D. ... or find my passion in life*
> *for that matter.*

Instead of spiraling into an abyss of depression, which somewhere in the dark recesses of my mind I feared might happen, I saw in my mind's eye a wave of water that had reached its peak and was now on its descent. It was as though I saw my thoughts and feelings in that instant as sloping brainwave frequencies. It was as if I had held my breath for the longest time and finally exhaled. And with this, I felt a strong undercurrent of calm and contentment. I couldn't remember the last time I felt this way.

> *Wait, what just happened?*

I had just lost my drive to continue my doctoral studies, the completion of which my entire identity and happiness seemed to depend on, and yet I wasn't feeling that bad?

The power came back on in my brain, and the wheels slowly started to churn again. Did the wave I saw represent the wave of my thoughts and emotions? It must have. I was sure of it. The moment I "gave up," the moment I finally let go of my burning desire to find my calling in life – my identity – I lifted the dam of desire and let the wave run its course and continue its onward descent.

I had experienced calming moments in my life before, but this one felt qualitatively different. It was much more satisfying. I would feel calm and happy when my life was going the way I wanted it to. But if anything went awry, I felt anger or profound disappointment. The new calm didn't lie meek and feeble at the mercy of the whims of external conditions. It was unconditional.

I leaned back in my chair and pressed the knuckles of my right hand hard against my lips and lay my folded left arm across my abdomen: I still feel anxious, I thought, that I no longer have a clear goal and plan. But my fingers aren't that fidgety. I still feel frustrated, no question. After all, I put my heart and soul into a project that I no longer care for. Yet the tire isn't completely deflated, so to speak. I still feel dejected that I failed, yet again, to find something I'm passionate about. Yet I'm not clenching my jaws or grinding my teeth.

There was something about that voice earlier. *It's okay ... I don't have to find my passion in life.* In the past, I never liked to feel pain. I mean, who would? Check that, I *despised* feeling pain. I would launch any such feeling from my heart and mind like a grenade. I wanted to sentence to death – by lethal injection – that feeling of nervousness and tension, depression and insecurity, as well as the feeling I just couldn't get anything right.

Today, I had a sudden change of heart. It was as though I could hear my mom's consoling whispers in that earlier voice. I heard the unspoken words of Master Daehaeng's soothing presence. I heard the complimentary cadence of Ms. Kim, my Pansori teacher. And I heard the earthy twang of the anonymous hockey dad I once met. I channeled all of these voices in my head, and this new collective voice put its hand on my shoulder and whispered, "S'okay, buddy. These feelings are natural; they're what make you human." Being okay with my emotions, steadying them in that split-second, was the trigger that lifted the dam and washed to shore my dire quest for purpose.

Split-second. My judgment of these emotions was so subtle, instantaneous that I failed to recognize there were, in fact, two layers of pain that existed in such moments: the raw pain itself – pain as is, if you will – and my reaction to it. This last train of thought was like a gust of wind that blew aside some of the fog in my mind.

Why did all this sound so familiar?

I remembered. *See into the true nature of things by seeing them as they are.* I came across this saying numerous times back in my Dongguk days, as well as in Master Daehaeng's books.

Did what I just experience reflect what the Zen masters meant by this?
Glen, do you know what this means?
It means you're an unforgiving bastard.

All these years, to think that I fancied myself a kind and caring guy. Perhaps to others, yes, but I wasn't nice to myself. I had unilaterally illegalized the act of being okay with my pain all these years. I was a ruthless dictator when I should have been a libertarian leader, by leaving the pain alone, not meddling in its affairs. By detesting the pain, I inadvertently empowered it. I armed the emotion with more weight and power than it really had. I antagonized it, poked it, instead of letting sleeping dogs lie. This gave the "sleeping" pain more life. I breathed dark life into it. I created an inner Frankenstein. Three inner Frankensteins, to be precise: anxiety, frustration and dejection, in bold block letters. That one instantaneous and subtle perception, that intense and negative judgment of my own emotions, further fueled my feelings of frustration or anxiety or dejection. Simply put, I made it worse for myself.

The wheels in my head were in full motion by now, and they started spitting out the analogies.

Yes, yes.

The moment I judged my emotions and thoughts was the moment I slammed down a dam wall on either side of what were naturally ebbing and flowing waves of thoughts and emotions. I stopped the waves in their path, grounded them to a halt, and rendered them stationary and inert, which went against their very free-flowing and dynamic nature. I cemented the pain into a noun when it was a verb. The Korean language was right: it should simply be "*love*," not "**I** *love* **YOU**." The trapped waves of emotions and thoughts festered and rotted there, in much the same way river water stagnates when it's not moving and flowing.

The moment I despised the wave of pain was the moment the mudslinger in me had cometh – my mind slung a fistful of mud at the middle or peak of the wave, the pain at its most intense and despised moment. Some mud stuck; some slid off. I carried the stuck mud around with me. The more I slung, the larger and heavier the mound became, until it dried and hardened into a sedimentary rock that entrenched itself inside. My heart grew heavy with its weight, until it became a part of me, my identity: it defined *who I was*.

No wonder I hated these painful emotions.
I identified with them too much …

To reinforce my insight, I continued to phrase it in various, although similar, ways, the thread zigzagging. The rock and the waves reminded me of a line from the *Tao Teh Ching*, which I read in my OM days. Lao-Tzu called the quality of rigidity the "company of the dead" and fluidity the "company of the living." When I muddied the peak of the wave of my thoughts and emotions, they became hard and rigid, and I had joined the company of the dead. That was true because I was dying inside. With a compassionate "S'okay, Glen" self-tap on the shoulder, however, I backed off of them and let them do their thing. I let the raw emotions and thoughts breathe and be. I allowed them to move in their natural state of constant fluidity. Instead of *who I was*, the pain was now something that was *happening* to me. I had re-joined the company of the living when this occurred because I felt more alive.

I then thought of a camera. The moment I reflexively judged the pain was the moment my mind's forefinger pressed down on the shutter button and took a snapshot of its peaking wave. It then became a still image, a powerful moment frozen in time in my head, with all the feelings and thoughts associated with that peaking wave. They lingered on and on in my head in all their glorious misery. But the moment I exercised a little self-kindness was the moment I let my forefinger go from the shutter button, and memories of those feelings and thoughts became more faint and less preoccupying as the wave descended.

The stack of logs lining one side of my cabin deck outside started to roll in my mind. Painful feelings didn't appear out of thin air as some fully formed, discrete and fixed "thing" from the outset, in much the same way I perceived the pieces of logs that I had delivered to my doorstep by the truckload every November. I suffered from tunnel vision then because I only saw LOGS, cylindrical pieces of wood that flailed in the air and landed on my dirt driveway while being unloaded. I snapped a still of them in my head and mentally froze them in time, blind to their previous and end forms. But these logs also had a story. They were also fluid. They had a beginning since they originally came from somewhere (trees). They had a middle stage, their current cylindrical form. And they would have an end (ashes) come December, January, February, March and possibly even April, since this was Ottawa.

In the past, then, I was a dictator, Dr. Frankenstein, a capitalizer and bolder of letters, a dam-builder, mudslinger and photographer all rolled into one. What I would do, to reprise a final time, is essentially take a moving part and try to make it sit still. I would take something fluid and turn it into a solid, as best as I could. I would try to kill fluidity for the sake of stability. In Taoist parlance, I would take something living and try to make it dead.

My mouth was dry. I got up out of my seat, poured myself a half-cup of water from the kitchen faucet and downed it. I walked over to Kitty, who was curled up in a furry ball on top of the folded towel that I had placed at the edge of the leather couch in the living room. I couldn't tell which side was her head and which was her tail. I gently stroked her back twice. *Purr.*

I walked back to my desk, sat down and crossed my arms. I was feeling at once exhilarated and numb. I was exhilarated at what I had just learned, but my mind was mush from what had just been a long unbroken chain of concentration. I lost perception of time.

17

Emptiness

It hit me almost two months later. I was cruising home on the highway one night from Morisset and, as usual, my mind was thought-hopping from one to another. *Emotions are novel each and every time they appear.*

My automatic trigger-response to past pain was to file it away, in my head, into a stale category called Anxiety. Or Dejection. Or Frustration. When my damp hands turned the door knob of the Pansori studio as I walked into my lesson, this was the same anxiety I felt when my fingers madly punched away at the keyboard minutes before the deadline at *The Korea Herald*: "Oh, brother – anxiety rearing its ugly head again."

When I lay down in my sleeping bag and stared into the utter blackness of the ceiling during SNU Orientation, this was the same depression I felt when I sat alone in my cabin in the woods and stared at a blank laptop screen: "Great – there's that feeling again."

When my brain bloated with floating ideas at Dongguk, this was the same frustration I felt trying to find my way through a labyrinth of acupressure points: "Fuck – the same old frustrated feelings ..."

But if anxiety is but a wave, since no two waves are created equal no matter how similar they look to the naked eye, then no two anxieties could be the exact same, could they? No two waves could ever be the exact same height, width and volume, not to mention the exact same combination of molecules of water, no? No two frustrations and feelings of dejection are the exact same for similar reasons.

That Ms. Kim would tell me to my face if and when my singing stunk was a clear and present danger to my pride and ego; the penalty for a cringe-worthy feature story at *The Herald* was, at worst, no more front-page stories for me – a First-World problem by comparison.

SNU's Orientation Week depression was the product of a longing to return home to Canadian innocence; cabin depression in Ottawa was the product of a longing for the rush of the rat race.

I was a frustrated astronaut spinning away into the abyss of abstraction at Dong-guk; I was a frustrated beginner climber looking up at Mount Oriental Medicine as a speck from the bottom of the mountain.

The possibilities in nuanced differences between each seemed many. The "raw materials" of this trinity of emotions were like Silly Putty and their manifested forms at any given time the products of delicate massaging and molding by the hands of our circumstances. Anxiety, Dejection and Frustration, as I knew them, began to lose their perceptual hold over me. Each were attached at the hip to the situation; there was no such thing as an isolated, objectified emotion, except in one's head. At best, I could say *frustration-in-that-situation* or *anxiety-in-that-situation* or *dejection-in-that-situation*, which was simply another way of saying *wave of frustration*, *wave of anxiety* and *wave of dejection*.

Items stored in my TBC bag for over a decade were now coming out one by one.

> *Is this what Master Daehaeng meant by "emptiness" when she said*
> *everything in our lives changes every moment?*
> *That all things manifest anew as time flows and spaces change?* [1]

Master Daehaeng's teachings become more real and relatable to me. Whenever I looked for bedtime reading material, my hands consistently gravitated toward her books in both Korean and English, which had been gathering dust all these years on my shelf.

One night I came upon the following passage:

> Why – all of you ate a meal yesterday, will you eat again today? Well, even eating a meal, there is nothing fixed about it. You eat this, you eat that, you hear this sound, you hear that sound, you see this thing, you see that thing, you go this way, you go that way, or you become a father, then a husband, then a brother, then a son-in-law – every single thing about you just naturally rolls along like this, yes? So when you become something, when you do something, when you think something, can you say "I" did it? There will be

---

1 Many years later, while taking a break from writing this very chapter, I became curious about creative writing, specifically how the mind works in the creative process. So I Googled "creativity." After perusing some of the links, I stumbled upon a 1996 *Psychology Today* article penned by noted psychologist Robert Epstein, entitled "Capturing Creativity." One passage in particular caught my attention, in which Epstein sounded more like a Zen master than a psychologist:

Behavior is generative; like the surface of a fast-flowing river, it's inherently and continuously novel. We never repeat the same action or have the same thought twice, at least not if you look closely enough. We brush our teeth a slightly different way each morning; we dream new dreams each night. If you say "dog" twice, a spectrograph will easily distinguish two patterns. Behavior flows, and it never stops changing.

nothing I can say I did. This is because everything about you rolls along without a fixed form.

As I was reading the passage, one by one the sentences grew more strident, first roping me back from the precipice of sleep, then dragging me down from the clouds of abstraction, and finally pinning me to the ground of the present moment. No need to harp on just emotions or their make-up, it was telling me. And there was nothing more to conceptualize. Emptiness was evident right here, right now, in just *being*.

18
No Self

"CHINESE FOOD?" I TEXTED STEVE ONE evening. I was done reading and writing for the day, and hard apple cider beckoned.

"Can never go wrong with that!" he texted back. "Meet at Loblaws for cider?"

"Read my mind," I texted.

"ETA?" he texted back.

"Bout 8."

"K. *Big Brother* tonight."

"Nice!"

That was what I loved about Steven Tomlins – he always kept his apartment doors open to his friends and his TV screen glued to reality shows. He gave me something to look forward to in the evenings, usually Monday and Tuesday. Come to think of it, we'd also meet Wednesday, Thursday and Friday evenings. Sometimes I'd go over both Saturday and Sunday night, too – why stop when you have a good thing going, I thought.

Steve was doing his Ph.D. studies on atheism in Canada at Ottawa U. We were a good match on many levels: he was of good Scottish-English-Irish-Norwegian stock while I was of good Korean stock. We were the same physical height (although he was much stockier), around the same age (I was four years older), preferred politically incorrect humor and came to Ottawa with lots of life stories. Actually, he took the cake. His story about once having to move out of a house in Barrie (north of Toronto) because bikers had taken it over – and turned it into an after-hours bar – made my experiences in Korea look like choirboy stuff.

Soon after Steve and I arrived at his apartment with ciders in hand, he got a text from a mutual friend.

"Hey," Steve said, looking up from his phone, "you up for going to a party later tonight?"

"Where?" I said.

"Patrick's, he's having some friends over; it's just down the street near the Mac's on Laurier."

"Uhh …" I said. "I'd rather just stay here and keep it low-key tonight, if you don't mind. Not really in the mood to socialize."

"You're never in the mood to socialize," Steve said, rolling his eyes. "You're so anti-social …"

I felt like Steve had just pricked my ribs with an acupuncture needle. Which then tapped an acupressure point that was causing my face to melt, kind of like that Nazi from *Raiders of the Lost Ark*.

"No, it's just that," I said, my voice trailing off and growing whinier, "you know, with the thesis hanging over my head these days … it's hard to have fun."

"Well, I'm cool either way," Steve said, shrugging his shoulders and returning his attention to the computer screen.

I was reeling because I was just called anti-social. I had worked for years in Korea to break out of my Northern Secondary School shell. I was a changed man. But now I had regressed to my younger introverted self? More than a decade's worth of hard work down the drain? I was quick to console myself, by rationalizing that True Me was an affable guy who liked going out, but I was currently in the throes of writing a thesis and didn't have the patience to engage in small talk.

"Before we order Chinese, I wanna quickly play you a clip of a singer I discovered the other day. She's pretty cool," Steve said.

"Oh, right," I said without looking up from my Iphone, mindlessly surfing the Net with an unimpressed look on my face. Not looking up from my cellphone while conversing was my way of telling Steve I was ticked off at him. I was sitting in my usual spot, Steve's white Ikea single-seater sofa, and looked up every so often to watch the video. But I couldn't let go of Steve's comments. I was locked into my own thoughts.

Then I remembered:

> *S'okay, Glayne. You're human.*
> *Who likes to be known as anti-human?*
> *Your reaction is natural.*

I steadied and stayed with my feelings of indignation and then released them in that moment as though they didn't belong to me but to the natural waves of the mind, to "naturalness" as I liked to call it, their rightful owner. And the moment I did so, I could swear that Indignation winked at me as it made its descent, as if to say, "You got me again, kiddo. You're getting good at this now." I felt lighter inside and was finally able to move past Steve's comments.

"So whatd'ya think?" Steve said, dragging the cursor to the "Back" icon at the top of the screen, ready to click on it once he heard my feedback.

The song was over. I had essentially missed the entire YouTube clip.

"I think, uhh, can you play that again? I missed some of it …"

I returned home a little past 11 p.m. that night. After I fed Kitty, I washed up, changed into my long johns and went to my desk and flipped open my laptop. I wanted to check my e-mail, Facebook page and the NHL news and highlights one last time before calling it a night.

As I waited for my laptop to power on, my eyelids came to rest halfway down my bulging eyeballs. I was exhausted. Yet I wasn't about to let those eyelids close all the way. I was fascinated that something as innocuous as a positive self-image could trigger such nasty emotions in me. That the "affable guy" self-image could suddenly cause a full-blown identity crisis.

To prevent further drowsiness, I didn't pluck my eyelashes *à la* Bodhidharma, the first patriarch of Zen, who was said to have done so every time he dozed off during his days-long sitting meditation sessions in a cave in China. I thought a less painful way would be to host a lively, albeit imaginary, debate in my head – between Chongwol Sunim, whose no-frills explanations I always found refreshing, as the Zen master and me as his young grasshopper:

> **Me**: And what's so wrong with forming a self-image that's positive like that?
>
> **Sunim**: Then it's man-made. It's made up in your head. It's an illusion, fiction. It's also mechanistic, a self-defense mechanism. It's not based in reality, and your experiences have shown you time and again that when you get in your head like that, you go down a slippery slope to suffering.
>
> **Me**: But I was having a bad day. Everyone does, and everyone acts out of character when they're not having a good day.
>
> **Sunim**: But that's just it. Why do you need to distinguish between a "bad day" and a "true me"? I'm not saying you're anti-social as if it was a permanent quality. Or even a social person underneath it all. I'm saying you don't feel like meeting lots of people at certain times in your life, nothing more, nothing less. It *happened* to you; it's not who you are. Remember? Stop making it worse for yourself. I'm trying to help you here. You seem to keep forgetting that I'm on your side.
>
> **Me**: Well …
>
> **Sunim**: And did you say out of character? That's a good one! Just because you have a bad day doesn't mean you're engaging and fun-loving underneath the anti-social veneer on that particular day. If you are, then where did that engaging-ness and fun-lovingness go on that bad day? If you can find them, bring them to me, and then

I will agree.[2]

Me: Well, they're not some physical thing, as if I can bring them to you. I just know I am, my essence, that is.

Sunim: You *think* you know. Or you *want* to believe you are that way because you crave certainty about who you are. How untenable and delusional a reason. C'mon man, you should know better than that – you're a Ph.D. student for crying out loud.

This last line was a cue to end the conversation. I removed the two interlocutors from my head and debriefed. It was making more sense. Self-image was like theory, an ideal. Idealizing the self was another name for rigid self-expectations. These expectations privileged what I thought was good and protested what I thought was bad, a kind of "should be."

I would mentally chariot around this self-image wherever I went. He was a bulky fellow who loomed in the shadows of my mind with folded arms, a figure that had grown, dried, molded and solidified into his present shape after 12 years in the Korean kiln: he loved meeting people, to have a good time, give speeches, banter, drink boilermakers and sing karaoke with his necktie wrapped around his forehead. By perceiving my feelings of indignation as but a flowing wave, I had nudged this figure out of the shadow and begun applying heat to it, and he was becoming more malleable. He was becoming someone who sometimes loved to have a good time, and sometimes not. Neither, I began to appreciate, were sewed to my soul.

I thought about my other long-cherished belief about my essence: being kind and caring. I situated it within Master Daehaeng's social roles example from back in the day. As a daddy, I offer my daughter help with a school project she's struggling with. After I finish helping her, I prepare a candlelit gourmet dinner for my wife, since it's Friday evening and I know she's had a long workweek. The next day, I go visit my parents, and I offer to pick up, on my tab, a month's worth of groceries for them on the way. That's *if* I really like my job and my boss, and my life is swimming along.

But if one of my co-workers spreads a malicious rumor about me in the office, or my boss chews me out in front of my colleagues one day, and the toxic work environment only escalates from there, I might just order in a large pizza for dinner the coming Friday (and get an early start on the wine), dwell on the despised co-worker/boss while simultaneously trying to help my daughter with her school project, and buy only one week's worth of groceries for my parents on my next visit (especially since I might be

---

2 This last line was inspired by the storied verbal sparring between Hui K'o, the eventual second patriarch of Chinese Ch'an and desperate for spiritual nourishment at the time, and Bodhidharma, the first patriarch:

Hui K'o said, "My mind is not yet at peace. Pray set it at peace for me, Master!"
The Master said, "Bring me your mind, and I will set it at peace for you."
Hui K'o answered, "I have searched for it, but in the end it is unobtainable."
The Master said, "Your mind has been set in peace."

out of a job soon). Or if I quit my job in disgust one day and storm out of the building with a box of my personal things under one arm, I'd probably walk right past the homeless guy by the main entrance doors who'd normally get all of the loose change in my pocket.

And these were only the obvious influencers; I was sure a subtle matrix of combinations and permutations of conditions could and had impacted my mood, thoughts and behavior on any given day. Or even one subtle condition, like the existence of mosquitoes in your room at night. As the African proverb goes, "If you think you are too small to make a difference, try sleeping with a mosquito." I had, numerous times in the cabin, and it made a difference. The following day, I would squint in disgust at the stinging rays of the sun, step on the gas pedal a little harder than normal, curse any car that didn't speed above 110 km/h on the highway, and regard with unbridled contempt conversational partners who beat around the bush before making their point. It was too bad cats didn't like to catch mosquitoes.

I wasn't the exact same kind and caring person all of the time. I could be kind and caring in different ways and to different degrees, or not at all, depending on my shade of mood.

Impermanence, impermanence, impermanence. Shades and shades and shades of grey. I was honed in on seeing the world that way now. I pushed my chair back, crossed my arms and lowered my gaze. It was nearing 2 a.m., and I was beginning to feel delirious.

"Let me get this straight," I slurred aloud to Kitty, who was curled up and fast asleep by my feet on the rug underneath the table. "Feelings are never the same twice … my personality is dependent on the context … man, I don't even know who I am anymore. Is this a mind-fuck or what, eh Kitty?"

Kitty's right ear perked up, the grey wisps of hair jutting out from the side of one of her ear lobes. It then gently folded back down. I knew what she was thinking: "here we go again, another one of his crazy rants."

19
Road Less Traveled

A YEAR AND A HALF LATER, I HAD MOMENtum on my side. Peter was okaying my chapters one by one (albeit with recommended revisions), and I was putting the finishing touches on the last few – the heart of my thesis.

I had re-oriented my entire research angle in that time. I had begun to see the interview data with fresh eyes, to link the dots in the data, to get out of my own way and let the data speak for itself, as Peter would often remind me to do. What I came to see were the contours of a pattern: the more "Koreanized" the Korean Buddhist participant was – that is, born and raised in Korea before immigrating, spoke fluent Korean while less comfortable with English, social circle was mainly co-ethnic Koreans, and so on – the more he/she took an interdependent approach to Buddhist practice and beliefs; the more "Canadianized" the participant was – born and raised in Canada, spoke fluent English and little Korean, social circle was mainly non-Korean friends, and so on – the more he/she took an independent approach to Buddhist practice and beliefs; and the more "middle-of-the-road Korean-Canadian" the participant was – spoke both languages relatively well, social circle was Korean and non-Korean friends, and so on – the more he/she took a balanced interdependent-independent approach to Buddhism.

Some of my department colleagues had warned me to start applying for jobs one full year before finishing the thesis – not after – because the hiring process could take up to another year. So I began preparing my applications. I Googled how to write effective cover letters and resumés for teaching positions and selected two or three chapters of my thesis that Peter had okayed to send as samples of my writing.

I next drew up a geographical priority list of the regions in the world to which I was willing to move for a teaching position:

1. The Canadian East Coast.

Yep, that was it. Okay, it wasn't much of a priority list, since this dramatically narrowed my university options to the four small Maritime Provinces of Canada: Prince Edward Island (PEI), Nova Scotia, New Brunswick, and Newfoundland & Labrador. The four had a *combined* population of under 2.4 million and only so many universities to which to apply. Most of my Ph.D. colleagues were open to moving to other parts of the world to teach. They were much wiser than I was. Supply was greater than demand and, as they say, beggars can't be choosers. I was well aware of this, but my propensity to visualize in HD Technicolor had just come out of retirement.

Although I had never visited the Maritimes, it was an idyllic hideaway in my mind's eye. I was particularly smitten with PEI, which coincidentally was Steve's hometown. It conjured up images of sweeping azure-blue oceanic vistas, dramatic sea cliffs, and rolling green hills and pastures, thanks to the tourism commercials and websites I had seen. The island was home to silky white sandy beaches that stretched along its shorelines as far as the eye could see and from which you could catch spectacular sunset views of the shimmering Atlantic Ocean.

It was littered with small picturesque towns, the cheery residents of which, I imagined, said "good morning" to you even if you were a stranger. And with farms with staked wooden signs by the dirt road that, in hand paint, announced "Fresh Baked Pies," "Sweet Non-G.M.O. Corn" and "Pick Your Own Strawberries." The unusual red and rich soil blanketing the island grew crops in abundance, and you could live off the fruits of your own labor. In fact, the very first image that sprung to mind when I thought of the province was rosy red-skinned potatoes. By the delivery truckload – I gorged on McCain's frozen French fries as a kid, and I knew they were made from PEI potatoes.

I had lived for over a decade under the glaring lights and within the tight spaces of Seoul, where my feet only touched pavement. I then moved back home to steel frames and glass office buildings in Toronto. And now I lived in Ottawa, Canada's capital and yet another (relatively) large urban space. I went from living with 10 million people to five million and now to one million. And I wanted to keep a good thing going. I wanted to shut off the noise, in my head and around me, and be surrounded by acres and acres of rolling hills and peace and quiet. With a total population of 145,000, PEI seemed like the ideal destination.

PEI also seemed like the safest place in the world to live and raise a family. I didn't hear a peep out of the province when it came to the evening national news and a breaking story about the latest appalling crime to hit Canada. (My hunch was confirmed a couple of years later when Steve texted me some of the day's top headlines from the front page of *The Guardian*, PEI's largest daily: it screamed "Burger Bust" when a uniquely PEI-style hamburger served with a scoop of ice cream on top was found to have 2,218 kilocalories and be very fattening; also residents were warned to remain vigilant as "Police seek PEI man for theft of Powerade bottle five years ago.") Moreover, I could actually afford to buy a place there, unlike some of the big cities like Vancouver and Toronto where the real estate prices were spiraling out of control.

I sent my application to every university and community college in the Maritimes, even if no position was officially advertised. I applied for the two or three full-time jobs that did come up with the minimum qualifications I met, and privately e-mailed chairs of certain departments to check if anything part-time might be available. I was willing and prepared to teach almost anything in my area of expertise, whether religious studies, East Asian studies, Canadian ethnic studies or Buddhist studies.

After months of waiting, I finally got a bite: it was the Religious Studies department at the University of PEI. A sessional teaching gig in the Winter semester, four months from now, was a possibility, they said. I immediately began looking into cheap and pet-friendly apartments in Charlottetown – PEI's capital – on Kijiji. As I did so, however, I kept reminding myself about the negatives of the position, as a kind of psychological self-defense mechanism, to cushion the blow in case I didn't get it: "This isn't a permanent full-time position, Glen, but part-time and semester to semester. There could be semesters where you have no work and so no money." Three months later, the department e-mailed me again: the funding for the potential sessional had fallen through due to "serious budget cuts." *Damn*. That one really stung. I only heard back from a few more institutions, who thanked me for my application but

> … at this time, we are not looking for PT instructors/you have not
> been selected to be considered for the next round of interviews.

I knew that one of my biggest drawbacks was that I didn't have any publications in academic journals or enough experience teaching undergraduate courses. I was intellectually drained from writing my thesis, and I didn't understand how my colleagues, Kyuhoon and Steve being but two, were able to pull off a journal publication or teach a course for a full semester while writing their dissertations.

I looked outside the world of postsecondary education and sent my applications to a private Buddhist high school and a Buddhist magazine in Nova Scotia, thinking these could possibly serve as interim work until I found a teaching gig in the region. Alas, notta – no available positions for the former, rejected by the latter. It was your classic case of unrequited love, institutionally speaking. I began to accept the fact that the Maritimes wasn't meant to be.

20
Passion

On December 20, 2013 – six and a half years after the day I set foot on University of Ottawa soil – my 320-page dissertation was done, and Peter gave me the green light to submit it to the Faculty of Graduate and Postdoctoral Studies (FGPS). It came down to the wire: today was the last day to submit before the university went on winter break.

I arrived on campus at 12:30 p.m. on the afternoon of December 20th with my cup of Tim Hortons in hand. It was minus-20 degrees Celsius outside, and the snow fell relentlessly from the ominous grey sky. In front of me lay vast clean blankets of snow with nary a footprint or tire mark. The students had already gone home for the break. The sounds of youthful chatter, laughter and reverberating car engines that could be heard only days ago had now stopped. The campus was an eerily forlorn and silent place today.

When I walked into Morisset, I was greeted by rows and swaths of empty seats. I noticed a couple of male students meandering through the hallways. I stomped my boots on the entrance rug, shook off the droplets of melted snow wedged in my hair and removed my gloves. I gingerly walked over to one of the many empty computer desks on the first floor, sat down, dropped my tote bag, and inserted my USB stick into the slot just below the computer screen. I wanted to give my thesis one last look. I wanted to check for anything glaring, before going downstairs to the photocopy center to print off four copies, as per the requirement. The time was now 1:14 p.m. I had plenty of time since the office closed at 5 p.m., although I was warned it could close a half hour earlier than usual when I called them yesterday. I didn't have a care in the world today, though. I was feeling relaxed and Bob Marley mellow knowing I would never have to read through another sterile journal article or tome again, or stare at a blank screen that screamed to be filled. I double-clicked on the file called "FINAL THESIS IN ENTIRETY."

"Ahhh …" I sighed to myself, "still can't believe I finished it …"

I slouched in my chair to get more comfortable and flippantly flicked the roll-bar of the mouse, expecting to skim through my thesis and only stop to correct the odd grammatical error.

"Hmm, this sounds a bit long," I said to myself as I leaned forward in my seat, put my left hand on my chin and stared at one particular sentence on page 3.

> It is also a religiously unique community insofar as its religious demographics are in stark contrast to the religious patterns in the homeland, where Buddhists comprise 25 percent, Protestants 20 percent, and Roman Catholics 7 percent of the population of Korea (Min 2010: 36), making them the three largest religions in the country.

It was long-winded. I deleted the comma between "homeland" and "where," put a period in its place and typed in "That is" after it.

Okay, that sounds a bit better.

"This, too …" I said after scrolling to the next page and finding a sentence that I wanted to break up into two.

On page 10, I spotted a sentence that required one more adjective to make it perfect: "applicable."

Ooohh, yes, that's much better.

I found something to "correct" every few pages. This went on and on, and I lost track of time. I looked up at the clock hanging on the wall on the far side of the room. It was 3:30 p.m.

Shit. Okay, stop, Glen.
No more.
It's good enough.

I quickly hit "Control-S" and exited the file. I leapt up from my seat, stuffed my USB stick into my pants pocket and barely managed to sling my bag over my shoulder. I rushed over to the photocopy center downstairs.

"Hi," I said, trying to catch my breath. "I'd like to print five copies of a file called 'Final Thesis in Entirety.'"

I handed the gentleman behind the counter my USB drive.

"Oh, sure," the man said.

"Uhh …" I said. "How long will this take?"

"Well …" he said, checking the clock, "it can probably be ready by about … 4:10?"

If the FGPS office closed at 4:30 today, this was going to be very close.

Why-o-why did I wait to the last minute to print?

There was no way I was going to postpone submission to the next semester. I had done this – and told my family "almost done" stories in the process – too many times before. I wasn't going to disappoint myself and others anymore. Besides, I'd probably pick apart my thesis some more if I did. And I refused to let my thesis hang over my head during the break and sully a fifth straight Christmas for me.

I also wasn't about to go sit down somewhere and wait because my heart was racing. I walked over to the campus convenience store to buy another cup of coffee. I paced the empty hallways while taking small intermittent sips. I returned to the photocopy center at 4:06. The copies were ready.

Yes.

I paid the gentleman, loaded the five copies onto my arms and rushed out the door. The FGPS office was across the street and a good 5-minute walk from the photocopy center but, in this heavy snow, it could take a little longer. When I stepped outside, I was blinded by the onslaught of snowflakes in my eyes. I couldn't see three feet in front of me.

As I trudged through the snow crunching beneath my feet, each step carried the weight of a block of cement like in a nightmare. I felt a stinging sensation in my fingers. I had forgotten to take out my gloves from my bag. I glanced down at my feet: the shoelaces on one of my battered black dress shoes had come undone, but I didn't have time or the hands to tie them. I was careful not to step on them, however, because there was no way I was going to drop the copies of my thesis in the snow. My thesis was way more important than a cracked head.

I arrived at the FGPS building and barely managed to pry open the thick wooden doors with the few fingers that were free. I briskly walked down one flight of stairs, mindful of my undone shoelace. When I saw a hand closing the doors to an office up ahead, I yelled, "Hi! Bonjour!" I was ready to lunge forward and toss flailing stacks of paper through the rapidly shrinking door opening if I had to.

"Oh, hi," said a pleasant-voiced, short silver-haired lady peering out from behind the doors with a bemused grin.

"Hi. Aw you cloze … ttt?" I said, stopping and panting and unable to clearly enunciate thanks to a half-frozen face.

"No, you still have a few minutes," the lady said calmly.

Her words and tone flowed into my ears and warmed my insides. I released the tension in my shoulders, and my heartbeat slowed.

"Are those copies of your thesis you have for us there?"

"Yes, how did you know?"

"Well …" she said with a sly smile. She must have seen this before, graduate students submitting their thesis at the last moment.

"I guess congratulations are in order."

"Thank you," I said, still feeling disoriented from the frenzy of the last five minutes.

I followed her down a short flight of stairs into the FGPS office. I plopped down the stacks of copies of my thesis on top of her desk.

Thud.

The *thud* echoed and lingered in the air.

That *thud* was it.

It was the sound of my passion in life found. I felt it in the humming in my chest. I smelled it in the raw freshness of the wet snowflake dripping from the tip of my nose.

Yet everything about this moment was anti-climactic and premature. The *thud* didn't sound like any blaring trumpets I heard. *It* was supposed to be the discovery of a career that I loved, and I would know this by the long and fulfilling days of work that preceded that moment. But the Ph.D. program wasn't a career, let alone an endeavor that I loved. The degree, which I had yet to officially earn (the final step was the oral defense in front of the thesis committee), would only confer the right to apply for a university teaching job. Incidentally, I also envisioned more fluttering confetti and friends and family smiling, woo-hooing, hugging and high-fiving me right about now. Instead, I was congratulated by a stranger, albeit one with a friendly smile.

I understood. It was anti-climactic because my passion was more bone than flesh. My passion was achievement itself. It was about running, cycling and swimming to the finish line of a grueling triathlon, whether I placed or not. About the doggedness to outlast a behemoth bully in a street fight where I was the last man standing, to make it back to shore after being swallowed by a rogue wave, to come out on top of an undertaking that challenged every emotional fiber of my being – my fears, my insecurities, my patience, my willpower, my stamina. About the resilience to ultimately slay a noble opponent – me. And with this did I, to paraphrase Thoreau, subdue and cultivate 10 ounces of flesh, pacify a heart that yearned to be set free this whole time, which, in turn, won me peace of mind. Not happiness. Peace of mind. The two were not the same. Happiness, to me, was a feeling that scratched the surface, while peace of mind underlay it, a deep and enduring layer.

I picked up a couple of cans of apple cider at Loblaws on the way home to celebrate, alone. Steve had already gone home to PEI.

"Meow!" Kitty yelped as soon as I came home and flung open the cabin doors.

"Yes, we did it, Kitty!" I said. I immediately bent down to hug and kiss her. I closed the door, and Kitty headed straight to her food bowl by the kitchen with her tail up; she knew the drill.

Even with the baseboard heaters running all day, my cabin felt chilly. I needed to get my fireplace going. I looked over and saw a stack of five thick and dry logs and a half-used bundle of kindling lying on the hearth, pieces of wood chips and log peels scattered underneath them. I was out of newspaper, though. Amidst the euphoria, I had forgotten to drop by the village convenience store for scrap newspaper on the way home. I had an even better idea, though: why don't I use the extra copy of my dissertation that I brought home instead? Not only would this save me a 10-minute trip, it would wipe my thesis – at least, its paper version – off the face of this earth.

As I squatted in front of my wood-burning fireplace with a half-drunk can of apple cider in one hand, I watched the typed black font on the pages of my dissertation slowly become enveloped by the fiery red of the flames. I remembered then what the Chinese Zen Master Lin-chi once said (and I'm paraphrasing here): "The only good use for textual stuff/analytical papers is to wipe your ass."

I understood that the dissertation didn't merely represent the last six and a half years of solitary drudgery and monotony. The tens of thousands of words on those 320 pages were seething with the anxiety, dejection and frustration of not only my thesis but also my many career attempts over the years. That's why it felt so damn good to burn it.

21
Full Circle

"Hi, Glen," the voice on the other end of my cell phone said.

I knew exactly who the voice belonged to. I felt something churn in the pit of my stomach. "Hey, Nanda," I said. "How are you?"

"Fine," he said.

Nanda Lwin was an old friend from Toronto, whom I first met when I helped out my sister at the post office, where he rented a postal box. Not only was he a second-generation Asian brother (of Burmese-Filipino descent), he was easygoing and laidback, and not unlike Steve, the same height as me but much stockier. My close friends all seemed to fit this psychological and physical profile. Funny how that works. Nanda and I kept in touch every so often while I lived in Ottawa.

In the past year or so, however, I had grown jealous of him: he was a tenured professor in the Civil Engineering department at Seneca College in Toronto who had taught for a decade now. Meanwhile, here I was, only a year younger and still desperate to find a teaching job after more than a year's worth of rejections. I had successfully defended my thesis a few months ago to make my degree official. What should have been a joyous occasion only served to remind me of the sobering reality of how little the degree actually offered. It was time to think in more practical and realistic terms now. The degree was only the beginning. I now needed to stand out in a crowded room of distinguished doctors of philosophy clamoring for attention. I was a single male adult on the sinking Titanic jostling with the hundreds of more-essential-to-save passengers to get on one of the rafts. The only way to have a *chance* at that seat was to publish, publish, publish. Preferably in esteemed academic journals, which didn't accept any old thing. But to publish would take yet another year, at the very least, and I didn't have the patience or strength. The Ph.D. wiped me out. Time, however, had no sympathy. I was 42 years old, and the march of time

163

stomped louder with each passing day.

"Well, I was looking at the Careers page on Seneca's website today," he said.

"Uh-huh."

"I found a position I think will be suitable for you."

I wasn't impressed. I was still pouting from the Maritimes experience and, more recently, I had been passively rejected – i.e., I never heard back – by a few other universities and colleges closer to home, in the province of Ontario. I was beginning to think it was useless to apply.

"Okay," I said, just to indulge him. "What's the area of specialization?"

I could hear the sound of a keyboard being punched on the other end of the line.

"Well, it says here you have to have a Ph.D. in anthropology ... or related field."

"But I didn't study anthropology."

"Yeah, but I think you should apply anyway," Nanda said, adding that courses at Seneca's School of English and Liberal Studies (SELS) tended to be broader than universities in breadth and that I could fit in very easily with an arts degree. I was naïve to how the "liberal studies" departments at vocational and technical schools operated. College profs here were apparently required to be more subject generalists than university profs, who were subject specialists.

"Oh, really?" I said. "And, you know what, my thesis did take an interdisciplinary approach ... including anthropological."

"You also have to have at least three years of teaching experience," he said.

"Three years?" I said. "Well ... if you combine the time I taught at U of T and Ottawa U., I meet that ... but barely."

"Anyway," Nanda said, "I think you should apply. I mean, it won't hurt to try ..."

I Googled "Seneca College Careers" and checked the posting for myself. When I scrolled to the bottom of the page, my doubts were confirmed.

"Oh, shit. The posting says internal candidates preferred."

"Yeah, so?" Nanda said defiantly. "That doesn't mean they won't hire an external candidate. Like I said, it doesn't hurt to try."

After we hung up, I begrudgingly double-clicked on my laptop folder called "Resumes," upon which a sea of blue and red Word and PDF files of past resumés and cover letters assailed my eyes. I squinted my way through them before selecting a cover letter and CV I had recently sent to another college in Ontario. I went to work on fine-tuning it, to square it with Seneca's job description. I was getting sick of this, but I told myself this would be the absolute last time. It wasn't until the wee hours of the morning that I hit the "Submit" button. I closed my laptop, went to bed and forgot about the application.

Two weeks later, I grabbed my usual cup of Tim Hortons coffee in the morning and drove to Morisset. I just wanted to get out of the house and continue scouring the Internet for more jobs from the comfort of the school setting.

I sat down in front of one of the computer desks on the first floor – going to the sixth floor triggered PTSD-like symptoms – and opened my Gmail account. An e-mail from Seneca had arrived in my Inbox. My heart started racing. I knew the news would be different from the previous rejection letters. I knew this because the reply came quickly; it took much longer to be rejected.

I clicked on the e-mail and, lo and behold, the School of English and Liberal Studies was inviting me to an interview. As soon as I clicked "Accept," I logged off the computer and headed outside, where my fingers fumbled to phone Nanda and Steve to tell them the good news. I didn't call my own family – my parents or sisters – because I didn't want to get their hopes up for the umpteenth time in case I didn't get the position. Besides, it was only an interview I was being invited to. I decided to remain low-key with them this time.

The 45-minute-long interview would be conducted the following week and involve a 10-minute teaching demo on a topic of my choice. This was a no-brainer: if there was one topic I was confident talking about, it was the roles that Korean and Canadian cultures played in the religiosities of the younger generation of Korean Buddhist practitioners in Toronto. The real challenge would be to condense more than 300 pages of soul-sucking academese into 10 minutes of lively and interesting talk.

I dusted off my old navy blue suit and pink tie that had been gathering moss in the closet and which beckoned for the iron. I felt like a modern-day caveman readying the razor, knowing his days living in a mountain cave were numbered, on the brink of once again rejoining civilization.

I met Nanda at Sheppard subway station in Toronto, on the day of. He was currently on summer holidays but offered to accompany me through the expectant maze of stairwells and hallways at Seneca to find the room I needed to get to. I was grateful because he would be my insurance policy against being late. If I was late, that would have sealed my fate even before the interview began.

We arrived on campus an hour before the scheduled time, so Nanda took me on a brief tour of the college, which sat on a chunk of prime real estate on the north-eastern edge of my old stomping grounds of North York, at the intersection of major arterial routes. The building itself was one elongated and connected set of multiple silvery grey low-rise buildings punctuated with bold red signage, the brand color of the school. Inside, an open-concept design dominated the larger communal spaces on the main floor, puncturing a hole up the middle of the two floors above it. The school felt larger than it was.

We arrived at the interview room on the ground floor of the "A" building 10 minutes early. I straightened out my tie a couple of times within the first few minutes. I then peeked through the glass panel next to the door. Up on the projector screen inside the room was an older and distinguished-looking gentleman. Likely another candidate who was being Skyped in, I thought. I could make out the backs of five heads in the audience staring up at the screen. I figured they were members of the interview panel.

Nanda turned to face me. "Are you nervous?" he said.

"Yeah a little bit …" I understated, with both my hands resting on top of my belt buckle in solemn embrace.

"But s'okay," I said with a smile.

It was okay because this was simply how I was feeling at this specific time and place. I reminded myself the feeling wasn't who I am.

"You'll do fine," he reassured me.

"I know," I said, smiling. "But thanks anyway ..."

I glanced at my cell phone a few minutes later and saw it was 1:25 p.m. My nerves returned. This time with a vengeance. They punched me right in the gut. My heart began to pound, my fingers began to fidget and my awareness of the present intensified. I sensed my brain and body were ready to launch into #Performance-Mode, and that was a good thing.

After 10 minutes had passed, a tall middle-aged woman with a mushroom cloud of fluffy blond hair opened the door.

"We're sorry for the wait," she said in a cheery voice. "C'mon in."

"Okay, thank you," I said. I turned to look at Nanda one last time.

"Knock 'em dead," he said.

I slowly made my way to the front of the classroom, turned around to face the audience and smiled.

There was something very familiar about this.

I had seen this before. I was at another Korean social gathering where I had to perform, or even at the small Pansori studio trying not to embarrass myself in front of the kids. But instead of 600 pairs of eyeballs or even 10, it was "only" five. Instead of improvising, I would talk about a topic I had labored over for the past six and a half years. Instead of singing in front of giggling kids more than half my age or a living human cultural treasure, I would talk to well-mannered adults about a rather obscure topic where *I* was the one with years of training behind me. And instead of Korean, I would speak in my mother tongue. I wasn't intimidated.

The woman who had opened the door took her seat and introduced herself as the moderator.

"So welcome," she said. She then introduced the rest of the members of the panel.

"We thought we'd switch up the itinerary we sent you and begin with the teaching demo, if that's okay with you."

"Sure," I said. I was ready to roll with the punches and show my stuff regardless of the order.

"Okay, great," she said. "Well, I have a timer here, and you'll be given 10 minutes, as per the instructions in the e-mail."

I went right to work.

"Hi, everyone," I said, clasping my hands as was my habit. "Well thank you all for taking the time out of your busy schedules to come here today and give me this opportunity."

"Since the e-mail said 'topic of my choice,' I thought I'd talk about what I know best, and what I know best is my thesis topic."

I saw some smiles in the audience.

One hour and two whiteboards full of sharp squiggly lines later, I came out of the interview room feeling like I was walking on water. This was easily the best interview I had ever done, job-related or not. It wasn't even close. I spoke clearly, confidently and fluidly during the demo and in each of my responses to the questions from the panel.

As I held my iPhone in my trembling hands waiting for it to power back on so I could call Nanda, only one thought crossed my mind: "I got the job."

One month later, I was in downtown Ottawa running an errand on a hot and muggy afternoon when my cell phone rang. It was Claire Moane, the Chair of SELS.

"Are you sitting down somewhere and ready to hear this?" she asked in a sweet voice that melodically floated into my ears.

"Yes ..." I said, my voice rising.

"Well, I just wanted to congratulate you and offer you –"

I felt the strong urge to cut her off mid sentence and say *You had me at congratulate!*

22
Kitty

I waited one morning in the lobby of the emergency animal hospital in Newmarket, a suburb just north of Toronto, a 30-minute drive from Seneca College.

I leaned against the hard plastic seat in the waiting area with my arms folded. The two administrators behind the counter were talking on the phone. A mother and daughter sat patiently on the far side of the waiting area with their leashed brown golden retriever, who was sitting on the floor, his eyes alert and attentive. The dog looked to be the model of health and happiness. *Wonder what's wrong with him?* I glanced over to the seat next to me, on my right, where Kitty's empty carrier rested. Tufts of dark-green towel spilled out from the bottom of the half-open metal cage doors. An old plastic nametag, courtesy of my Ottawa veterinarian, hung sideways from the top of the cage. I tilted my head to read it: "Kitty Choi," it said.

Twenty minutes later, a lady in light blue veterinarian scrubs came out through the swinging doors in the back.

"Hi," she said in a lowered voice.

I stood up to shake her hand.

"I'm Dr. Daniella Shmuel. Are you Kitty's owner?"

"Yes," I said.

"Why don't we sit down for a moment."

I moved Kitty's cage to the floor space in front of me.

"Can you tell me how long Kitty has had diarrhea?"

"Uhh, for about a week now."

"I see. Now, she has a severely distended stomach, and –"

"Okay," I interrupted. I didn't want to hear what she had to say after the "and." Although I had only a vague idea of what "distended" meant, I didn't like the sound of it. "I did notice she looked a little bloated, more than usual. I thought she was just gaining weight."

"Unfortunately, it's quite serious."

Pause.

"Now we don't know the exact cause. We would have to run more diagnostics. It could be cancer, it could be something lodged in her stomach, we're not certain. But this will take a lot of time, and we might be looking at thousands of dollars in costs. She would also most likely require surgery, and Kitty's at an age when she might not survive it."

I sat there with my mouth open.

"How old is Kitty again?"

"She's 16," I gulped.

"You know, Kitty's suffering now, and she's lived a nice long life, I'm sure, and –"

My eyes suddenly welled up. A tear streamed down my right cheek. The day I had dreaded for years had arrived like a ton of falling bricks.

"Oh, dear," Dr. Shmuel said, turning her face away for a second. She turned to look at me again, this time with tears in her eyes. "This is the part of the job I hate. Would you like some tissue?"

She handed me a couple of pieces from the box at the counter. "Why don't we move to a private room?"

I stood there in one of the private treatment rooms. Dr. Shmuel started speaking. But her words drifted like echoes in the distance. I was feeling numb. In my heart, I knew she was right. It was time to let go. Kitty had lived with Irritable Bowel Disease since she was seven, which brought her nothing but tens of trips to the local animal hospitals, where she was subsequently poked, prodded and injected. She was denied, for the most part, the pleasure of eating chicken and beef for the latter half of her life. I fed her a steady prescription diet of duck and venison and green peas. I gave her canned salmon and tuna only as a treat. Still, there were multiple setbacks, at which time I had to force-feed her steroid pills. And now she had something else, something that looked far more serious. She had suffered enough, and it would be very selfish to try to keep her alive any longer.

Dr. Shmuel carried a blanket-wrapped Kitty into the treatment room and onto the stainless steel table. She left me alone with her. I would tell Dr. Shmuel when I was ready for the euthanization. Kitty's eyes relaxed as she rested her chin on her right paw, her usual pose before falling asleep. She was probably thinking this was but another routine check-up. Little did she know. I stroked her knowing this would be the last time. I repeated to her how much I loved her and how grateful I was she was there for me whenever I was feeling lonely or sad in my Ph.D. years.

Dr. Shmuel returned to the room 15 minutes later and prepared the IV needle and tubes.

"She won't feel a thing," she promised.

Pause.

"Okay?" she whispered.

I nodded. As the fluid made its way along the tube, I continued to stroke the back of Kitty's head and whisper in her ear, "You're such a good girl, Kitty. Do you know that? You're such a good girl …"

When I returned home from the hospital, there was no Kitty to greet me at my door – for the first time in seven years, but it seemed like my whole life. I dropped Kitty's empty cage down in the middle of the floor of my studio apartment. I walked over to my bed, sat down at the edge and lowered my head. I saw, on the floor, patches of Kitty's white fur knitted into the light beige carpet. I looked up and around the room. There was Kitty's favorite sleeping spot beside the hearth of the electric fireplace, at the center of a coil of loose TV cable wires, where she felt protected by its circle. Over in the kitchen sat a bowl of half-eaten duck and pea kibbles and a full bowl of water I had freshly poured this morning.

The room turned dim, as though a cloud had moved into the sun's space. The air was dead and dull. Deafening silence. The room was lifeless, like some wasteland. More silence … The achievements, the insights, the validations and the joy – my life – flashed before me in successive snapshots … and collapsed to the floor from their perch. These all seemed insignificant now, even pathetic. And I could no longer hold back the rush of tears.

23
The Collective

One evening, during my first year of teaching at Seneca, I was in my office marking tests when I heard the unmistakable clicking noise of mopping outside my office.

That must be the cleaning person, I thought.

Putting down my red pen, I took this as a cue to go for a washroom break. I locked the door behind me and, as soon as I rounded the corner, I made eye contact with the cleaning lady. She was a young woman of East Asian descent.

"Hi," she said in a cheery voice as she stood up straight. She was wearing the aqua blue uniform shirts of Seneca's custodians.

"Hi," I said. I introduced myself.

"Oh, I'm Pina!" she said in a thick Chinese accent. Somewhat surprised, I asked her whether "Pina" was a typical Chinese name.

"My Chinese name is Yiping," she said as she leaned on her mop, "but sounds like Pina, like Pina Colada in English, so I choose Pina!"

In my mind, I thought the connection here was vague at best, but I let it go.

"I used to work in maintenance at a supermarket," I said, trying to find common ground between us.

"What is maintenance?" Pina said, squinting her eyes and tilting her head sideways.

I had to take another approach. "I mean I used to clean washrooms and floors."

Pina looked like she had just seen a ghost. "Now!?"

"No, no," I said. "I mean a long time ago."

Her tightened facial muscles relaxed as she broke into a wide grin.

"Oh, yeah, okay ..."

We chatted for a couple more minutes before we went our separate ways.

I returned to my office and picked up my red pen, only to slowly put it back

173

down. Seeing Pina with her tussled hair and mop stick in hand triggered memories of my time at Whole Foods 10 years ago. I fondly recalled the invigorating physical exercise, the good times bantering with my co-workers, and learning about the new and exciting health products on the market. On the other hand, I was very glad to leave when I did.

I remembered how physically and mentally taxing it was to come to work at Whole Foods day after day: getting down on my hands and knees to scrape the remnants of a squashed raisin off the floor in the bulk foods section; mopping, dusting and wiping until my hands felt arthritic; and scrubbing the mess on public urinals and toilets left by others. Pina could not possibly enjoy her work, despite her cheery exterior, I thought. I imagined she was working as a custodian because she had to. I had learned that she was a recent immigrant to Canada, and I knew that newcomers with an international education had to earn or upgrade to domestic academic credentials just to be considered for certain kinds of employment.

I suddenly saw my U. of Ottawa degree with fresh and appreciative eyes. I wondered whether Seneca would have even considered my application had I earned my doctorate abroad, which could have conceivably happened had I stayed in Korea. Plus, I couldn't forget I might have been rejected by Ottawa U. had I not written my Master's thesis in English. I felt a sudden sharp pang in my stomach: success and happiness seemed so random and fragile.

I started to sink into an abyss of reflection. I thought about my parents. I grew up in a middle-class family that could afford to send me to Korea to study all those years and pave the way for me to earn a Ph.D. Without my doctorate, I wouldn't have met the minimum qualification to even apply for the Seneca position.

Ah, yes, that Ottawa U. degree ...

Without Peter's patient and reassuring guidance, I truly wondered whether I could have finished. I had heard horror stories about doctoral students who met the "wrong" thesis advisor – professors who were aloof in their guidance and yet unfairly demanding of their students – and later switched universities, advisors or thesis topics, or quit their programs altogether after having invested three, four or five years of their lives in the dissertation project. Would I have had the inner fortitude to keep going had I met the "wrong" advisor? Probably not. I was at a very fragile and vulnerable place in my life at the time, and meeting that kind of an advisor could have broken me.

I shifted my attention to Seneca. If Seneca hadn't recently mandated more Ph.D. hires, my position would have been quickly filled by one of the many veteran internal candidates at the college; I doubt I would have even been invited to an interview.

I thought about the courses I was teaching. I'd lost that lovin' feelin' over the years while studying in Ottawa, that feeling of excitement, being alive, and virtue rewarded. Until, that is, it was brought on back by my first semester of classes at Seneca. Classes averaged between 20 and 30 students, an ocean removed from the hundreds registered in most of the classes for which I guest-lectured and T.A.-ed at the University of Ottawa.

At Seneca, I got to walk up and down the entire width and length of the class-room while talking about my interests, such as Eastern vs. Western cultures and Buddhism, without the need for a mic. I was able to look at each of my students in the eye. I could ask them questions that received plenty of answers (except for my Monday morning and Friday afternoon classes). I could joke and laugh with them. I wondered whether I would've experienced these small joys teaching at the university level.

I transitioned into thoughts about returning home to Toronto. My mind gravi-tated to a recent family get-together to celebrate Heejeh's birthday at the local Man-darin buffet restaurant. I saw the wrinkles curl up around the sides of my mom and dad's eyes and the frown lines form on their foreheads as they strained their ears and squinted their eyes to understand the rapid-fire English banter and jokes between Orion, Robin (Heejeh's father-in-law), Roy and my two sisters.

The expression on my parents' faces mimicked mine during my first few years at SNU. I felt their pain: they felt like outsiders unable to join in on the group-bonding thanks to those pests called slang and cultural frame of reference. Their exposure to other Canadians and Canadian culture occurred at Crosstown Discount Variety, where a typical exchange with their customers included "Hi," "That's $1.26 with taxes" and "Thank you, bye."

Unlike the first few years at SNU, however, this time I had the power to do some-thing to remedy the situation: I interpreted the back-and-forth into Korean as swiftly and best as I could. When my parents' wrinkles and frown lines finally gave way to smiles and teeth, that one moment alone almost did justice to the entire 12 years I spent in Korea learning the language.

My parents left the cultural comforts of Korea to immigrate to Canada and bore decades of cultural and language- and work-related hardships just so their three kids could have better economic and social opportunities than they did. The wrinkles and frown lines that I saw creased around my parents' eyes and over their foreheads that evening were physical scars from decades' worth of this pain. To come back and live in Toronto was to be gifted with these precious opportunities to appreciate them more and repay a fraction of my indebtedness to them; they were now in their 70s, and such opportunities grew fewer with each passing year.

I thought about my nephews – 9-year-old Kian, 6-year-old Rory and 3-year-old Ben. I'm no longer that vague familiar-looking uncle from Ottawa they saw a couple of times a year, in the summer and at Christmas. That has been a boon for me more than for them. Seeing them more often has been like free therapy: I thought about their cherubic smiles, their zest for the little things in life we adults take for granted (such as how good a freezie can taste and make you feel), and their sponge-like ability to pick up new words and expressions in one listen – "No, Uncle Glen … you never listen!" 3-year-old Ben once admonished me after I didn't properly follow the rules he had carefully laid down for a game he had invented.

The therapeutic moments extended beyond my nephews. I've since reminisced and shared a few laughs over a pint or two with my cousins John and Peter about our hockey playing days and those nasty judo classes. I've since reconciled my jealousy of Nanda now that we were colleagues (ironically, thanks to him), and I've begun the long road to paying him back for finding me the Seneca job with a few juicy steak dinners.

Then there was my buddy Barth. After losing touch for 12 years, Facebook reunited us. He, too, had moved back to Toronto only a few years ago after living in New York for several years as a journalist for a music magazine. When I saw him again, memories that had been hitherto boxed up and locked away flooded into my head. I didn't realize how much I had missed him. We took a stroll down memory lane, literally, visiting our old stomping grounds, including Northern Secondary, and going for a banquet burger at good ol' Burger Shack, which was still in business after 35 years. And their burgers still produced the same satisfied looks on our faces. We were naïve and innocent back then. We thought we had the world figured out and in the palm of our hands. And, yet, I looked back on those times with only fondness because our youthful exuberance was of the unsullied and pure kind, something we would never forget.

I shuddered at the thought I would've missed out on so many precious new memory-making moments had I found work in the Maritimes, a place my myopic eyes once envisioned would fulfill all of my needs and wants.

My thoughts finally returned to Pina Colada. She was a reminder to be grateful, grateful for the collective effort it took for me to be where I was today, that I got this teaching position at Seneca not because of "me, myself and I" but because of a slew of factors that were *beyond my control*. Come to think of it, she also served as a reminder, albeit indirectly, to be grateful for not getting exactly what I wanted because what I wanted was not what I needed. To borrow Hui K'o's words, a matter is fortunate in reality, although its form appears unfortunate. There was some "greater reason." I had to connect the dots to realize it.

Epilogue

"No soup."

My theories have found new life. I have another passion project. This time, I envision myself working with family, friends, and like-minded people and volunteers who have come together to run and live at a retreat center *cum* organic hobby farm in a small town in the country. One to two hours from Toronto by car. And this time, I'll be going in with a little more wisdom.

So during the week, I'd teach at Seneca, and on the weekends I'd be on the farm,

in my overalls, wearing a straw hat, with dirt under my fingernails.

On one particular Saturday afternoon, I harvest vegetables from a row of raised beds. An hour later, I move to another row, where I begin digging, planting seeds and seedlings, and covering the area with mulch, which included recycled weeds.

I sit back for a moment, wipe the sweat off my brow with my wrist and take a moment to survey the land. I am awe-inspired by the vast expanse of the open green field, the endless string of cedar rail fencing and the sea of towering sugar maple trees encasing it. The air is filled with fragrances.

The scorching heat is testing my patience and determination. For the third time this week, I tell Barth, who is kneeling next to me, that I think he is skimping on the mulch. He throws up his hands, stands up and says *then you do it!* I'm taken aback. *I'm just trying to help you, Barth*, I say in a calm voice. He takes off his gloves, breathes deeply and walks away toward the greenhouse, the familiar taut muscles along his chiseled jawline bulging. Where did that come from? I think. Talk about sensitive. Now I feel enraged and frustrated.

I engage in an inner dialogue: *S'okay to be pissed, buddy. Remember, it's only an emotion, a very natural one.* The wave of frustration passes. I experience the nature of my emotion as not a static noun that represents *who I am*, but a flowing verb that is *happening to me*. I take a long and slow breath. Perhaps Barth is right about me. I can be obsessive and a perfectionist about how things should be done. I decide to go and apologize to him for micromanaging, that I do it without realizing I'm doing it.

As I get up from my crouched position, I feel the pain in my back and hear the cracking of my knees. I whisper under my breath *man, I'm getting old.* Yet, as grueling as the work is, I feel the days here are long, productive and fulfilling.

I reach the greenhouse. When I apologize to Barth, he concedes he also responded in an automatic way, not allowing the wave to flow.

Several minutes later, with a pail full of carrots and chickpea pods in one hand, I open the door to my solarized, off-the-grid mobile modular home, one of several that dot the length of one side of the field, each bought by their respective owners. I am greeted by a tongue-wagging Rover, my Golden Retriever dog, while Kitty the II, my new Tortoise Shell Persian cat, takes this opportunity to escape outside through the slightly ajar door.

My wife, whom I met through a local dating website for farmers, comes out of the study room to give me a peck on the cheek. She tells me there's good news and bad news. The good news, she's almost done designing the website for the farm-retreat center. The bad news, the local municipal government has turned down our request for a permit to build another barn.

Dammit. The first barn was a red century-old equestrian horse stable that we retrofitted and now use as the communal kitchen, as well as a BnB with several guest rooms. The second barn was going to be our beautiful conference center, a place to host our public events ranging from yoga and Buddhist meditation retreats to workshops on sustainable living and DIY alternative health modalities. My knees grow weak. I sense my original vision is about to come crashing down.

I then remember that my mind is myopic. Perhaps the greater reason for this is ... we are overextending ourselves with this retreat center idea, and we should just stick to farming, which is difficult enough as it is. Or we could further renovate the current barn to make space for a conference room. Maybe I am being too greedy in wanting *two* barns. Whatever the case, I tuck these thoughts into the TBC corner of my heart, keep my gaze steady and forward, and trust that the dots will connect in the end. Besides, I think to myself, I have learned a lot about issues in zoning and land development in this process, which I believe will benefit me in some invaluable way down the road.

My wife and I wash up, go outside and walk hand-in-hand along a rolling dirt pathway leading to the communal kitchen. We pass a curving pond with a single pink lotus flower floating at the center. On the other side of the pond is a family of free-range chickens bobbing their heads as they scurry along.

I see a procession of Team B members – Nunes, Roy, Heejeh and Orion – bring out from the kitchen a large bowl of beet salad and pots of steamed rice, lentil soup, curried cauliflower and potatoes, and kimchi. Nunes proudly tells me that most of the dinner ingredients came from our crops and that dessert will be homemade pecan pie. I see my mom and dad seated at one of the long wooden picnic tables, and they have already started on the eating. *Don't forget to donate any excess veggies to the local food bank*, my mom reminds me. My dad chuckles heartily just before putting a spoonful of soup into his mouth.

The earlier permit rejection is still pricking the back of my head as I eat. I'll have to let the other co-managers know about this after dinner. *Ugh*. Our whole vision rested on this second large building.

It would have been perfect. I can't seem to let go of the idea.

I put my fork down. I project myself way into the future, to my own death. On my deathbed, I ask myself, what will I think when I am lying down and look back at this time, when I wasn't able to get the zoning permit? I think about this for a moment – I will have more pressing concerns. This heap of flesh of mine will soon be reduced to earth, water, fire and wind, and I will forever be forced to let go of my hold over the retreat center in the process. What I accomplished (and didn't) will be nothing but sound and fury at death. I will hold dear to me my loved ones all about, but peace of mind will come from somewhere else. What will matter the most is something intangible – that I stared down my heart and mind, and lived my life to the fullest as a result. That is what I will savor in my last heaving breath.

I chuckle inside and shake my head at the absurd comedy that is life. I release the tension in my shoulders and neck.

After dinner, we all sit around the wraparound deck drinking locally made Ontario wine while watching the sun set. We share stories and laughs while the musically inclined among us sing and play the guitar, banjo, and harmonica. I sing some Pansori as well.

I get up and walk to the kitchen to fetch another bottle of wine. I come across Kitty the II stretched out on a spot on the deck where the last rays of the sun are shining from the West. She lets out a mouth-splitting yawn.

I smile … *yes*, I whisper to myself.

NOTES

CHAPTER 7: A MANTRA IS BORN

page 50 "pull the weeds and bury them near the plant": Suzuki, S. (1991). *Zen Mind, Beginner's Mind: Informal Talks on Zen Meditation and Practice*. New York: Weatherhill.

page 50 "common mode of living": Thoreau, H.D. (2014). *Walden and Civil Disobedience*. New York: Vintage Books.

CHAPTER 10: ABSTRACTIONS

page 69 Venerable Pi Mo Yen of Wu T'ai Shan Monastery used to carry: Yuan, T. (compiler), and Ogata, S. (translator). (1990). *The Transmission of the Lamp: Early Masters*. Wolfeboro: Longwood Academic.

page 73 A man was giving his wife a kiss: Daehaeng Kun Sunim. (2011). *The Furnace Within Yourself: Dharma Talks by Seon Master Daehaeng*. Anyang: Hanmaum Publications.
    Master Daehaeng often used the example of the inherently diverse roles of a person in his/her daily life to clarify the Buddhist concept of emptiness. My recollection of the exact words she used when I first heard her explanation in the late '90s is vague. This particular passage, which was said by Master Daehaeng in one of her Dharma Talks in 1989, comes closest to my memory of her words, tone and explanation at the time. Note on the translation: I have taken the liberty of making a few slight changes to the translated English version as I saw fit.

page 74 All the world's a stage: Shakespeare, W. (1998). *As You Like It*. New York: Dover Publications.

CHAPTER 11: IMPERFECT PITCH

page 80 Some die sitting: My thanks go to the *Hanyeongdaeyeok Badibyeol Jeonjip* project, whose English translation of Maestro Park's version of *The Song of the Red Cliffs* I referenced while translating this particular set of lyrics. Any errors in translation are my own.

For the project's translation of Maestro Park's version in its entirety, see: Choe, T.H. et al. (2011). *Hanyeongdaeyeok Jeokbyeokga Badibyeol Jeonjip 1, Bak Dong-jin Version Jeokbyeokga*. Jeonju: Shina. Retrieved from seoulstages.wordpress. com/2012/03/15/pansori-lyrics-in-english-for-free.

CHAPTER 12: IN THE TRENCHES

page 97 Hwang has composed and produced four albums: Choi, G. (2000). Hwang Byung-ki: Riding with the Legend. *The Korea Herald*, Dec. 29, 2000.

page 109 Dear Spirit, since such is the cycle of life: Hanmaum Seonwon. (2002). *Sinhaengyojeon*. Seoul: Donguinswaesa.

This particular passage is my own English translation of one small section of the *Musang-gye*, the entire Korean-language text for which can be found in the aforementioned book. Any errors in translation are my own.

page 110 "enmeshed," "estranged": Epstein, M. (1995). *Thoughts Without A Thinker: Psychotherapy From A Buddhist Perspective*. New York: Basic Books.

CHAPTER 16: EBB AND FLOW

page 140 "company of the dead," "company of the living": Tzu, L., and Wu, J.C.H. (translator). (2005). *Tao Teh Ching*. Boston: Shambhala.

CHAPTER 17: EMPTINESS

page 144 Behavior is generative: Epstein, R. (1996). Capturing Creativity: How to enhance the creativity of a person and figuring out the mysteries of the creative process. *Psychology Today*, July 1, 1996. Retrieved from www.psychologytoday.com/ us/articles/199607/capturing-creativity.

page 144 Why – all of you ate a meal yesterday: Hanmaum Seonwon. (2005). *Heogongeul Geonneun Gil: Gungnaejiwonbeopoe 2*. Anyang: Hanmaum Publications. This passage is my own translation of the original Korean text; any errors are my own.

CHAPTER 18: NO SELF

page 150 Hui K'o said, "My mind is not yet at peace.": Yuan, T. (compiler), and Ogata, S. (translator). (1990). *The Transmission of the Lamp: Early Masters*. Wolfeboro: Longwood Academic.

CHAPTER 20: PASSION

page 160 subdue and cultivate ... of flesh: Thoreau, H.D. (2014). *Walden and Civil Disobedience*. New York: Vintage Books.